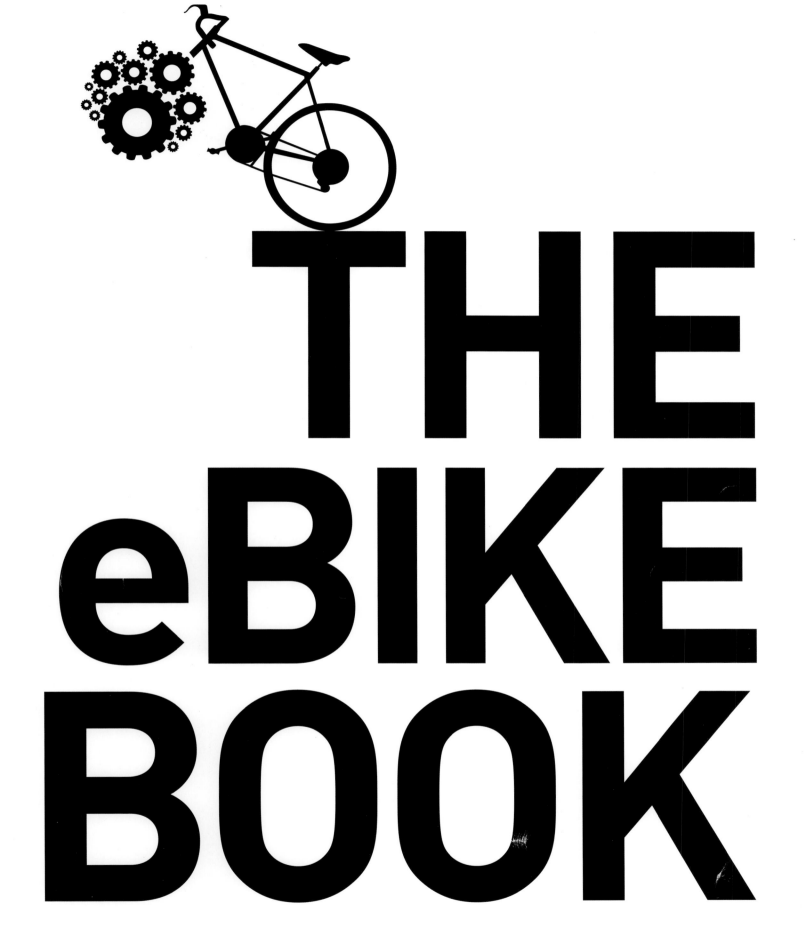

THE eBIKE BOOK

teNeues

CONTENTS

FOREWORD

FUTURE MOBILITY

E-BIKE HISTORY

TECHNOLOGY

10 REASONS WHY E-BIKES ARE COOL

PRODUCTS & PORTRAITS

RIGHT BIKE FOR YOUR TYPE

GLOSSARY

CREDITS & IMPRINT

WHEELS OF POWER

Bicycles are experiencing a global renaissance. There are certainly many reasons for this, most significantly the trend toward "electronification." This enhancement makes the bike an acceptable means of transportation for nearly everyone. A perfectly logical idea—or so you would think. And yet, many people in industrialized nations view the bicycle as a piece of sports equipment intended just for fitness freaks, and they overlook its great potential for "convenience." In emerging economies, on the other hand, bicycles are considered the poor person's means of transportation, only used by those who can't afford a car.

To fully appreciate the advantages of the e-bike, you need to take it out for a test ride. A true bicycle/motorcycle hybrid, this vehicle is neither entirely one nor the other. The e-bikes that dominate the market are properly termed pedelecs (PEDal ELEctric Cycles). What sets them apart from a hybrid is that the rider can choose between muscle power and electric power—that is, they operate as either a bicycle OR a motorcycle. The motor provides assistance only while muscle power is being applied.

Since 1993, mass market pedelecs have been available in Japan, which led the market for many years. This situation changed in the late 1990s when rapid sales growth in China left all other markets in the dust. Today, around 150 million electric two-wheelers are on the road in the People's Republic. However, it's vehicles that run completely on electric power that dominate the Chinese market. In Europe, on the other hand, pedelecs did not gain popularity until the 21st century, with the Netherlands leading the way. The pedelec gained acceptance here because they make everyday biking easier, and the Dutch appreciate the bicycle's functionality more than its potential as sports equipment. Other European markets, such as Germany and Switzerland, didn't experience significant sales growth until 2008.

For most people around the world, owning an e-bike will become as commonplace as having a cell phone over the next 20 years. Two decades ago, few people felt the need for a cell phone, but today these mobile devices are such a permanent part of daily life that it would be unthinkable to do without them. This trend continues to grow, due to the extensive range of smartphone functions available. Just as short-range thinking at the executive level of tele-communications providers initially prevented mobile phones from outpacing landline business, the bicycle industry also continues to largely underestimate the pedelec's potential. It remains to be seen who will dominate the market 20 years from now. Probably, the situation will closely resemble the IT sector today, where the once dominant manufacturers of mechanical writing implements have been pushed aside.

In a study for Bosch back in 2008, I predicted that 250 million new pedelecs would be sold on the market by 2050. By comparison, around 160 million bicycles are currently being sold each year. The sales strategy will be a crucial factor in meeting this prediction, or even exceeding it, a scenario which I now believe is more likely. One possibility would be to have a sales model similar to the one used for mobile phones. Using this approach, e-bike users would pay a usage fee and a symbolic purchase price of one dollar.

I hope you will enjoy reading this entertaining and educational book. In addition, I encourage you to visit your local bicycle shop and take an e-bike out for a test ride. It will help you understand and actively "experience" the material discussed in the book.

Hannes Neupert

Das Fahrrad steht vor einer weltweiten Renaissance. Diese hat sicherlich viele Gründe, doch ein ganz entscheidender ist die „Elektronifizierung", die es so aufwertet, dass es fast jeder Mensch als adäquates Fortbewegungsmittel akzeptieren kann. Eigentlich logisch, sollte man meinen. Ist es aber nicht – weil für viele Menschen aus Industrieländern das Fahrrad als Sportgerät für die aktive Freizeitgestaltung gesehen wird und eine Verbindung mit „Bequemlichkeit" noch eher verpönt ist. In wirtschaftlichen Schwellenländern hingegen gilt das Fahrrad als Arme-Leute-Verkehrsmittel für diejenigen, die sich kein Auto leisten können.

Erst mit einer Probefahrt erschließt sich die Dimension dieses Verkehrsmittels, welches ein echter Hybrid aus Fahrrad und Motorrad und doch keines von beiden ist. Die E-Bikes, die den Markt dominieren, werden fachlich korrekt Pedelecs (PEDal ELEctric Cycles) genannt. Das Besondere ist, dass man sich nicht wie bei einem Hybrid zwischen Muskelkraft und elektrischer Kraft, also Fahrrad ODER Motorrad, entscheiden kann. Der Motor unterstützt nur im Zusammenspiel mit der Muskelkraft.

Seit 1993 gibt es Pedelecs in Serie auf dem japanischen Markt, der viele Jahre der führende war. Seit Ende der 90er stellen die Verkaufszahlen in China alles andere in den Schatten – heute fahren rund 150 Millionen elektrische Zweiräder auf den Straßen im Reich der Mitte. Dort dominieren jedoch die Fahrzeuge, die man auch rein elektrisch fahren kann. In Europa hat das Pedelec seinen Siegeszug erst in den 2000er-Jahren angetreten. Der Impuls kam aus den Niederlanden, wo die Bevölkerung das Pedelec annimmt, weil es das Radfahren im Alltag leichter macht und das Fahrrad dort mehr ein Gebrauchsgegenstand als ein Sportgerät ist. Erst ab 2008 konnten auch in anderen Märkten wie Deutschland und der Schweiz nennenswerte Stückzahlen verkauft werden.

Das E-Bike wird für die meisten Menschen auf dieser Welt in den kommenden 20 Jahren so normal werden wie der Besitz eines Mobiltelefons heute. Auch wenn vor 20 Jahren die Mehrheit ein Handy nicht vermisst hat, heute ist es – nicht nur in den Industrienationen – fester Bestandteil im Alltag der meisten Menschen und nicht mehr wegzudenken. Dieser Trend verfestigt sich aufgrund des Funktionsumfangs des Smartphones noch weiter. In den Chefetagen der Telekommunikationsanbieter wurde der Mobiltelefonie nie die Chance eingeräumt, das Geschäft mit dem Festnetz zu überflügeln. Ähnlich geht es dem Pedelec heute in der Fahrradindustrie: In seinem Potenzial wird es noch weitgehend unterschätzt. Es bleibt abzuwarten, wer den Markt in 20 Jahren dominieren wird – wahrscheinlich wird es ähnlich sein wie in der IT-Branche heute, in der die ehemals dominanten Hersteller der mechanischen Schreibgeräte-Industrie verdrängt wurden.

Ich habe schon 2008 in einer Studie für Bosch die Erwartungshaltung geäußert, dass im Jahr 2050 jährlich 250 Millionen Pedelecs neu in den Markt verkauft werden. Zum Vergleich: Heute werden rund 160 Millionen Fahrräder jährlich verkauft. Entscheidend für die Realisation dieser Prognose oder sogar ihre Übererfüllung, die ich aktuell für wahrscheinlicher halte, ist die Verkaufsstrategie. Hier bietet sich ein Verkaufsmodell wie bei Mobiltelefonen an: E-Bikes sollten über eine Nutzungsgebühr und einen symbolischen Kaufpreis von einem Euro erhältlich sein.

Ich wünsche Ihnen bei der Lektüre dieses unterhaltsamen und zugleich lehrreichen Buchs viel Freude und empfehle Ihnen unbedingt eine Probefahrt bei Ihrem Fahrradhändler – zum besseren Verständnis und zum aktiven „Erfahren" der Materie!

Hannes Neupert

FUTURE MOBILITY

GLOBAL CHALLENGE

REDEFINING TRANSPORT

||||||||||||||||||||||||||||||||||||||||||||||||||||||||||||||||||||||||||||||||||||||||||||||||||

Our world is facing tremendous demographic and climate policy challenges. The Foundation for World Population predicts that the ten billionth person will be born in the year 2050. The process of urbanization is continuing unabated, and medium-sized cities are developing into mega cities at an ever faster pace. In China, which has a population of 1.3 billion, 2011 marked the first time that more people lived in cities than in the country. The twenty largest cities in the world are home to approximately 280 million people.

Suburbs spring up surrounding large cities, and people begin to commute between the suburbs and city centers. Everyone wants and needs to be mobile. This applies in particular to emerging countries, where populations and economic growth have doubled in recent decades.

Developments in rural areas show a sharply contrasting scenario: Regions are being abandoned, local public transportation is being reduced due to the drop in demand, and as a result mobility is limited for the mostly elderly population that remains. At the same time, global problems are on the rise—climate change presents us with tremendous challenges—yet political countermeasures are often not far-reaching enough.

Many cities are facing issues such as traffic congestion and air pollution. The notorious traffic jams in Moscow are a symptom, because too much private transportation is concentrated in a limited area. Traffic jam is "probka/пробка" in Russian, and it means the same thing as "cork." It is a fitting image to describe the situation on the streets: Even four-lane sections of highway become bottlenecks due to the high number of cars. Every year, Berlin residents spend an average of 69 hours in traffic jams, and residents in Warsaw average as many as 106 hours.

To get the associated problem of air pollution under control, many European countries are establishing low-emission zones where only low-emission cars can drive. Other cities, such as London, charge high tolls to use inner city streets.

Beijing takes it one step further: On certain days, only cars with license plates ending with an even digit can drive, while on other days only those with plates ending in an odd digit. Rich Chinese citizens simply buy two cars—one ending with an even and one with an odd license plate number. In Beijing, new registrations are limited to 20,000 per month, while the number of applicants is 50 times higher than that. This results in a situation where used cars are actually more expensive than new cars, since they already include registration, and you can avoid the uncertainty of the license-plate lottery. Shanghai also limited the number of new license plates just a few years ago, and there they are simply auctioned off. As a result, the current price for a new license plate currently comes to the equivalent of $13,000. With this system, Shanghai raised enough money in just a few years to construct an extensive state-of-the-art subway network. Starting in 2013, the license plates for electric vehicles will be free of charge, which will presumably result in a boom for electric vehicles.

Unsere Welt steht vor großen demografischen und klimapolitischen Herausforderungen. Die Stiftung Weltbevölkerung erwartet die Geburt des zehnmilliardsten Menschen im Jahr 2050. Die Urbanisierung schreitet voran, mittelgroße Städte entwickeln sich immer schneller zu Megacitys. In China, das 1,3 Milliarden Einwohner hat, lebten 2011 erstmals mehr Menschen in der Stadt als auf dem Land. Die 20 größten Städte weltweit beherbergen etwa 280 Millionen Menschen.

Dazu entstehen Schlafstädte in der Umgebung, von denen aus die Menschen in die Stadtzentren pendeln. Jeder will mobil sein, jeder muss mobil sein. Das gilt vor allem für die Schwellenländer, in denen sich sowohl die Bevölkerung als auch das Wirtschaftswachstum in den letzten Jahrzehnten verdoppelt haben.

Ländliche Gegenden entwickeln sich gegensätzlich: Regionen veröden, der Nahverkehr wird aufgrund der rückläufigen Nachfrage abgebaut und dadurch wird die Mobilität der zumeist älteren zurückbleibenden Bevölkerung eingeschränkt. Gleichzeitig wachsen die globalen Probleme – der Klimawandel stellt uns vor große Herausforderungen, doch politische Gegenmaßnahmen sind oft nicht weitreichend genug.

In vielen Metropolen drohen Verkehrsinfarkte, zudem haben die Städte zunehmend mit Smog-Problemen zu kämpfen. Der berühmte Moskauer Stau ist Symptom, wenn zu viel Individualverkehr auf einem begrenzten Raum stattfindet. Stau heißt auf Russisch „probka/пробка" und ist gleichbedeutend mit „Korken". Ein treffendes Bild für die Situation auf den Straßen: Selbst vierspurige Streckenabschnitte werden angesichts der Automassen zum Nadelöhr. Jeder Berliner steht im Schnitt jährlich 69 Stunden im Stau, die Warschauer kommen sogar auf 106 Stunden.

Um dem damit einhergehenden Problem der Luftverschmutzung wieder Herr zu werden, richten viele europäische Städte Umweltzonen ein, die nur mit schadstoffarmen Autos befahren werden dürfen, andere Städte wie beispielsweise London erheben hohe Mautgebühren auf die Nutzung der innerstädtischen Straßen.

Peking geht sogar noch einen Schritt weiter: An bestimmten Tagen dürfen nur Autos mit geraden Endziffern auf dem Kennzeichen fahren, an anderen Tagen sind die ungeraden Nummernschilder an der Reihe. Reiche Chinesen leisten sich allerdings einfach zwei Autos – eines mit einer geraden und eines mit einer ungeraden Zahl auf dem Nummernschild. Die Neuzulassungen sind in Peking auf 20.000 pro Monat limitiert, die Zahl der Bewerber liegt um ein 50-Faches höher. Dies führt dazu, dass Gebrauchtwagen teurer als neue Autos sind, da bei ihnen die Zulassung inklusive ist und man so der Nummernschildlotterie entgeht. Schanghai hat ebenfalls schon vor ein paar Jahren die Anzahl der neuen Nummernschilder limitiert, auch hier werden sie einfach versteigert. Die Folge davon ist, dass ein neues Nummernschild heute bis zu umgerechnet 10.000 Euro kostet. Mit diesem Geld hat die Stadt in nur wenigen Jahren ein weitreichendes modernes U-Bahn-Netz gebaut. Seit 2013 sind Nummernschilder für Elektrofahrzeuge kostenlos, was voraussichtlich zu einem Boom von Elektrofahrzeugen führen wird.

NEW ENERGY POLICY

BEYOND OIL

Internal combustion engines that rely on oil are what power the majority of our cars and cause high CO_2 emissions due to the reaction that occurs between carbon and oxygen during combustion. Together with other greenhouse gases such as methane, CO_2 accumulates in the Earth's atmosphere and prevents the heat from the sun trapped on Earth from radiating back out into space. Just like in a greenhouse, the Earth is heating up. In addition to the factory farming of livestock and the logging of forests that absorb CO_2, traffic congestion is just one of many factors that affect climate change, though it is by no means insignificant.

For cities that have committed themselves to climate protection and are attempting to reduce CO_2 emissions, traffic is the one aspect that is most difficult to control. In the majority of cities, emissions are continuing to increase because, although many cars are low-emission and have a green sticker, they still frequently emit more CO_2 than their predecessors due to the trend of buying vehicles that are heavier, such as the ever-popular sport utility vehicle.

Yet fossil energy sources such as oil and gas are limited. Experts estimate that oil production will decline between 2040 and 2050. Even if new technology makes it possible to extract oil more cost-efficiently, the reserves are still finite. Engines that rely on fossil fuels to function (gasoline/diesel) will have to be operated using different methods in the future. Even if internal combustion engines become increasingly efficient, the development of alternative drives is progressing slowly.

Science and industry are researching solutions and developing new mobility concepts. How can everyone be mobile without this desire bringing the world to economic collapse? How can this goal be fully achieved without restrictions on transport timing and location, while transporting people safely and independent of weather conditions? In Germany, everyone is talking about the new energy policy. It has to be implemented as quickly as possible. Renewable energies from the wind, water, sun, and biomass have to replace fossil and nuclear energy production. German politician Hermann Scheer described the new energy policy—in other words, supplying one hundred percent of power generated using renewable energy sources—as the greatest human cultural achievement since the industrial revolution. The objective is to supply all traffic with power generated from renewable energies. Many cars are in the testing phase, and the number of local rental projects and charging networks is growing.

Conventional bicycles are the most frequently used alternative to cars. Approximately 160 million bicycles are produced every year. To compare: In 2011, "only" around 60 million cars were manufactured. Bicycles have the advantage that they are accessible to almost everyone, and you don't need a driver's license to ride one. They save space, they consume very little energy in production and operation, and they have minimal maintenance costs. The downside is the limited range and the physical effort required, particularly when it comes to hilly areas or when riding into the wind. Although cars are more comfortable and designed for longer trips, they are more expensive to purchase and maintain.

E-bikes have tremendous potential to close this gap between bicycles and cars, and to function as transport for distances between 2 and 19 miles. They are significantly more comfortable than normal bicycles, and represent an excellent alternative for some of the distances traditionally covered using cars. Electric cargo bikes are helping small farmers and businessmen in emerging countries connect to traffic networks, providing them with a better way of transporting goods and, thereby promoting economic development and prosperity.

Die meisten unserer Autos fahren mit Verbrennungsmotoren auf Erdölbasis und verursachen einen hohen Ausstoß des Gases CO_2 durch die Reaktion von Kohlenstoff und Luftsauerstoff bei der Verbrennung. Zusammen mit anderen Treibhausgasen wie Methan steigt es in die Erdatmosphäre und verhindert, dass die durch die Sonne aufgeheizte Erde ihre Energie ins All abstrahlt. Wie in einem Treibhaus wärmt sich die Erde auf. Der Straßenverkehr ist neben Viehwirtschaft und Abholzung von CO_2-bindenden Wäldern nur einer von mehreren Faktoren, jedoch kein unbedeutender.

EXAMPLES OF PEAK OIL PREDICTIONS (CONVENTIONAL AND UNCONVENTIONAL)

Sources: Federal Institute for Geosciences and Natural Resources (BGR),
Hanover: Energy Resources 2009; Bundeszentrale für Politische Bildung

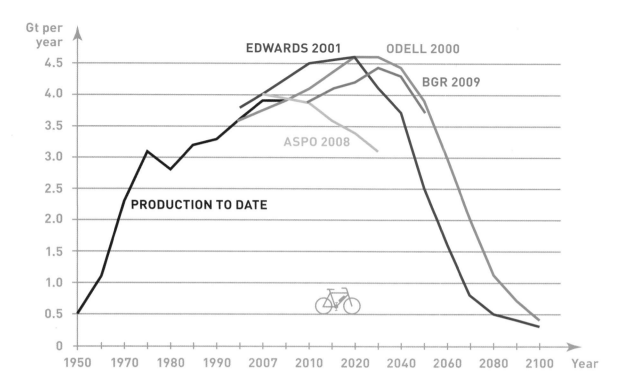

Für Städte, die sich dem Klimaschutz verschrieben haben und versuchen, die CO_2-Emissionen zu reduzieren, ist der Verkehrsanteil aber der am schwierigsten in den Griff zu bekommende. Immer noch steigen die Emissionen in den meisten Städten, denn viele neue Pkws sind zwar schadstoffarm und haben damit die grüne Plakette, um in die Innenstädte fahren zu dürfen, emittieren aber trotzdem oft mehr CO_2 als ihre Vorgängermodelle aufgrund des Trends zu immer schwereren Fahrzeugen wie dem beliebten Sport Utility Vehicle.

Doch fossile Energieträger wie Öl und Gas sind begrenzt. Experten schätzen, dass zwischen 2040 und 2050 die Erdölförderung zurückgehen wird. Auch wenn neue technische Verfahren zu einem ertragreicheren Abbau führen, sind die Vorräte dennoch endlich. Motoren, die auf Erdölbasis (Benzin/Diesel) fahren, müssen zukünftig anders betrieben werden. Auch wenn Verbrennungsmotoren immer sparsamer werden – die Entwicklung alternativer Antriebsmöglichkeiten schreitet nur langsam voran.

Wissenschaft und Industrie forschen an Lösungen und entwickeln neue Mobilitätskonzepte. Wie ist es möglich, dass jeder Mensch mobil ist, ohne dass dieser Wunsch die Welt zum ökologischen Kollaps führt? Wie geht das uneingeschränkt zu jeder Zeit an jedem Ort, und zwar sicher und wetterunabhängig? Die Energiewende ist in aller Munde, sie muss so schnell wie möglich herbeigeführt werden. Erneuerbare Energien aus Wind, Wasser, Sonne und Biomasse müssen die fossile und atomare Energiegewinnung ablösen. Der deutsche Politiker Hermann Scheer bezeichnete die sogenannte Energiewende, also die hundertprozentige Versorgung mit erneuerbaren Energien, als die größte menschliche Kulturleistung seit der industriellen Revolution. Ziel ist es, den gesamten Verkehr mit Strom aus erneuerbaren Energien zu speisen. Viele E-Cars sind in der Testphase und die Zahl an lokalen Verleih-projekten und Ladenetzen wächst.

Die am häufigsten genutzte Alternative zum Auto ist das klassische Fahrrad. Rund 160 Millionen werden pro Jahr produziert. Zum Vergleich: 2011 wurden „nur" rund 60 Millionen Pkws hergestellt. Fahrräder haben den Vorteil, dass sie fast jedem zugänglich sind und kein Führerschein nötig ist, um sie zu fahren. Sie sind platzsparend, verbrauchen weder in der Herstellung noch im Betrieb viel Energie und weisen minimale Unterhaltskosten auf. Nachteile sind die begrenzte Reichweite und die körperliche Anstrengung, speziell bei hügeligem Geländeprofil oder bei Gegenwind. Autos sind zwar bequemer und für weitere Strecken ausgelegt, jedoch teuer in Anschaffung und Unterhalt.

Das E-Bike verfügt über ein großes Potenzial, diese Lücke zwischen Fahrrad und Auto zu schließen und als Fahrzeug für Strecken von 3 bis 30 Kilometern zu fungieren. Es ist deutlich komfortabler als ein normales Fahrrad und eine gute Alternative für einen Teil der Strecken, die bislang mit dem Auto zurückgelegt werden. Elektrische Lastenfahrräder verhelfen Kleinbauern und -unternehmern in Schwellenländern zu einem Anschluss an Verkehrsnetze, ermöglichen ihnen einen besseren Warentransport und fördern so die Entwicklung der Wirtschaft und des Wohlstands.

FUTURE GROWTH

THE RISE OF THE E-BIKE

Do you know someone who rides an e-bike? A growing number of people are trying to conserve gasoline by walking or riding a bike. By making that choice, they are countering rising energy costs, the financial and economic crisis, as well as the threat of climate change. Commuting to work accounts for the majority of the ground people cover every day. Many users state that commuting is the reason why they purchased an e-bike.

E-bikes are purchased most frequently in China, followed by Europe with its leading markets of Germany and the Netherlands. The Dutch are considered to be the trendsetters in Europe when it comes to mobility, and two-wheeled mobility in particular. E-bikes currently enjoy a market share of 10% in the Netherlands. In the first half of 2011, Dutch bicycle dealers earned more than 50% of their revenue from e-bikes alone. Developments in the Dutch market are a strong predictor of developments for Europe. Since 2008, the European market has recorded annual growth rates of 50%. In 2010/2011, the sales of e-bikes exceeded the one million mark in Europe. By 2018, experts on lightweight electric vehicles predict annual sales of 1.5 to 3.25 million electric bicycles in Germany alone. This would represent a tenfold increase in market volume within just a few years.

In the meantime, nearly every well-known bicycle manufacturer offers an e-bike in their product line-up. Companies such as Panasonic, Yamaha, Magna, Bosch, Continental, Marquardt, Samsung, Höganäs, and Migros are investing heavily in drives, high-profile vehicles, and infrastructure. The fact that automobile manufacturers such as Porsche, Smart, BMW, Daimler, Audi, Opel, Toyota, Peugeot, Honda, and Volkswagen are also working on electric bicycles or have already introduced models on the market shows the importance they attach to them for future mobility.

Kennen Sie jemanden, der ein E-Bike fährt? Immer mehr Menschen versuchen Benzin zu sparen, indem sie zu Fuß gehen oder Rad fahren. Damit begegnen sie den steigenden Energiekosten, der Finanz- und Wirtschaftskrise und nicht zuletzt dem drohenden Klimawandel. Gerade das Pendeln zum Arbeitsplatz macht einen großen Teil der täglichen Wege aus. Viele Nutzer geben Pendeln als Kaufgrund für E-Bikes an.

Am häufigsten werden E-Bikes in China gekauft, dann folgt Europa mit den Leitmärkten Deutschland und Holland. Die Niederländer gelten im Bereich Mobilität und vor allem Zweiradmobilität als Trendsetter in Europa, hier haben E-Bikes aktuell bereits einen Marktanteil von 10 Prozent, holländische Fahrradhändler machten im 1. Halbjahr 2011 mehr als 50 Prozent ihres Umsatzes mit E-Bikes. An den Entwicklungen auf dem holländischen Markt lassen sich Entwicklungen für Europa gut ablesen und voraussagen. Seit 2008 verzeichnet der europäische Markt jährliche Wachstumsraten von 50 Prozent. 2010/2011 überschritt der Absatz von E-Bikes die Eine-Million-Marke in Europa. Bis zum Jahr 2018 prognostizieren Leichtelektrofahrzeug-Experten einen jährlichen Absatz von 1,5 bis 3,25 Millionen Elektrofahrrädern allein in Deutschland. Dies entspräche mindestens einer Verzehnfachung des Marktvolumens in wenigen Jahren.

Inzwischen hat nahezu jeder namhafte Fahrradhersteller ein E-Bike im Angebot. Firmen wie Panasonic, Yamaha, Magna, Bosch, Continental, Marquardt, Samsung, Höganäs und Migros investieren in großem Stil in Antriebe, imageträchtige Fahrzeuge und Infrastruktur. Dass auch Autohersteller wie Porsche, Smart, BMW, Daimler, Audi, Opel, Toyota, Peugeot, Honda und Volkswagen an Elektrofahrrädern arbeiten oder schon damit auf dem Markt sind, zeigt, welche Bedeutung ihnen für die künftige Mobilität beigemessen wird.

EUROPEAN COUNTRY E-BIKE SALES, 2008–2015*

*2013–2015 ESTIMATED

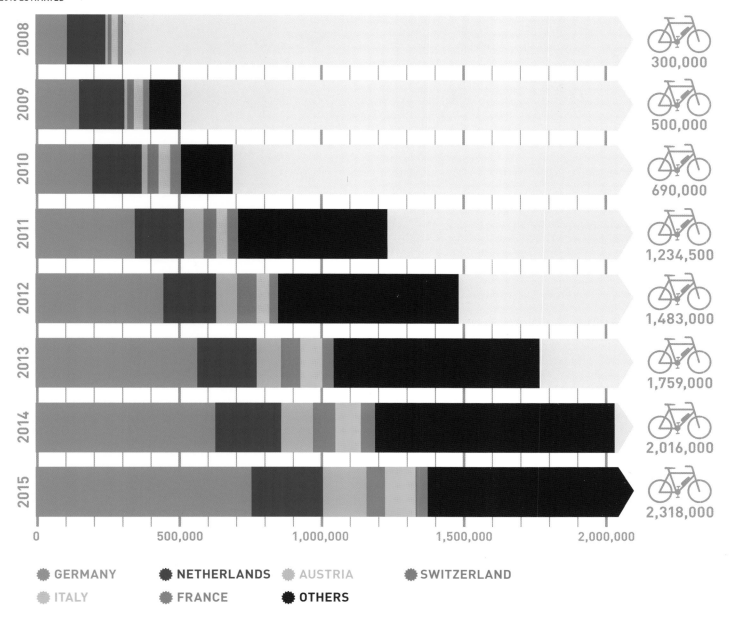

Year	Sales
2008	300,000
2009	500,000
2010	690,000
2011	1,234,500
2012	1,483,000
2013	1,759,000
2014	2,016,000
2015	2,318,000

● GERMANY ● NETHERLANDS ● AUSTRIA ● SWITZERLAND
● ITALY ● FRANCE ● OTHERS

WORLDWIDE E-BIKE SALES 2012

SOURCE: ELECTRIC BIKES WORLDWIDE REPORT (EBWR) 2013

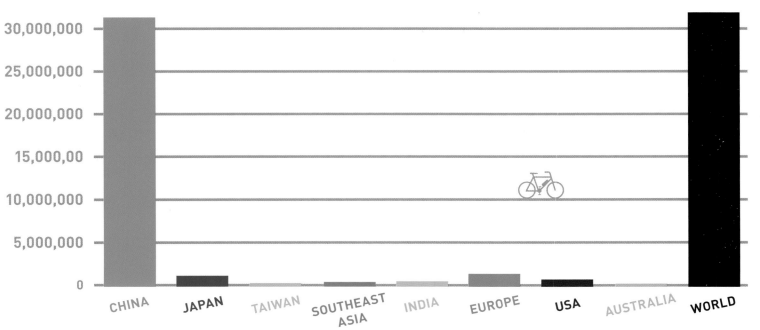

CHINA   JAPAN   TAIWAN   SOUTHEAST ASIA   INDIA   EUROPE   USA   AUSTRALIA   WORLD

CHANGE IN IMAGE

MOVING STATUS SYMBOLS

In China, e-bikes have already become everyday vehicles. Tax advantages for electric bicycles were put into place at the end of the 1990s. In the years leading up to that point, two-wheeled vehicles with internal combustion motors had become an emissions problem for the cities. As a result, taxes for motorcycles were drastically increased overnight, and the government offered various Chinese companies a one-time subsidy equivalent to approximately $130,000 to develop an e-bike. In Chinese factories, annual production rose from 58,000 in 1998 to 30 million in 2011.

Yet for most Chinese citizens, e-bikes represent only one step up the hierarchical ladder of motorization on the way from a bicycle to a compact car. Cars or at least motorcycles remain the desired status symbol: They are the trophies of success and symbols of prosperity and wealth. Currently only two percent of the Chinese people own a car; according to estimates by the Hamburg Institute of International Economics, that percentage will exceed ten percent by 2020. For a long time, photos of endless lines of bicycles shaped the European view of China. Today anyone considered to be an environmental polluter in the West—because parts of the Western world are becoming aware of the fact that fossil fuel sources are finite and that using internal combustion engines for private transportation is sheer lunacy—would be considered just a normal guy in China. It will not be easy to change the reputation of bicycles as something "backwards" in Chinese minds, improve their image and maintain their ubiquity.

In the future, the challenge will be to make e-bikes the preferred means of transportation for the masses in the BRICS countries (Brazil, Russia, India, China, and South Africa). These emerging countries have to find solutions to fulfill the desire of their citizens for individual mobility without adding to the already high level of CO_2 emissions. Unlike in China, in India electromobility had not attracted any interest for many years; instead, public buses, taxis, and rickshaws were operated using natural gas. In 2010, however, the central government began specifically promoting the industry and launched the National Mission for Hybrid and Electric Vehicles.

Chinese manufacturers of e-bikes have also recognized the trend and are planning to introduce European e-bikes in China as a means of appealing to the upper class. For image reasons alone, members of the upper class don't dare be seen in this type of vehicle because everyone knows how cheap they are. A similar situation existed in Europe in the 1980s, when it was taboo for business people to ride to work on a bicycle. This attitude only changed when mountain bikes came on the scene, because it became widespread knowledge that mountain bikes were expensive. For that reason, it was obvious that you weren't riding a bicycle because that was all you could afford, but rather because it was a healthy way of life.

Even in long-industrialized nations, it is important to change the image to that of a trendy vehicle. In Germany, bicycles with electrical assistance were long considered to be vehicles for senior citizens. That reputation still lingers. The development of new models is an important part of changing the image from that of a retiree bicycle to a fashionable vehicle. Both the growth of the market and product differentiation show how e-bikes have established themselves among various target groups. Thanks to new types of e-bikes such as mountain bikes, tandems, and cargo bikes, electric bicycles are of interest for active individuals, young families, and small businesses. Those over the age of sixty will continue to represent an important sales market; however, the emergence of innovative designs and powerful motors are announcing a clear trend.

In addition, the change in image is being reflected in the price consciousness: China, the Netherlands, and Germany are showing a rise in the average price for e-bikes. There is less demand for cheap products, and, particularly in Europe, consumer willingness to spend an average of over $2,000 for an e-bike is increasing. By contrast, the average price in Japan and the United States is less than $1,300.

In China hat sich das E-Bike bereits als Alltagsgefährt durchgesetzt. Ende der 90er-Jahre wurden Elektrofahrräder steuerlich bevorteilt. Zweiräder mit Verbrennungsmotor waren in den Jahren zuvor zum Emissionsproblem für die Städte geworden. Die Steuern für Motorräder wurden deshalb über Nacht drastisch erhöht und für die Entwicklung eines E-Bikes bot die Regierung unterschiedlichen chinesischen Firmen einen einmaligen Zuschuss von umgerechnet ca. 100.000 Euro. Die jährliche Produktion in chinesischen Fabriken stieg von 58.000 (1998) auf 30 Millionen (2011) an.

Dennoch erscheint das E-Bike den meisten Chinesen nur als Stufe auf der Motorisierungshierarchieleiter auf dem Weg vom Fahrrad zum Kleinwagen. Das erstrebenswerte Statusobjekt bleibt das Auto oder zumindest ein Motorrad: Sie sind die Trophäen eines erfolgreichen Lebens und Zeichen von Wohlstand und Reichtum. Aktuell besitzen nur zwei Prozent der Chinesen ein Auto, im Jahr 2020 soll der Anteil nach Schätzungen des Hamburgischen Weltwirtschaftsinstituts auf über zehn Prozent steigen. Bilder von Fahrradkolonnen prägten lange das europäische Bild Chinas. Wer bei uns als Umweltsünder gilt, heute, da sich Teile der westlichen Welt der Endlichkeit von fossilen Brennstoffen und des Irrsinns von Verbrennungsmotoren im Individualverkehr bewusst werden, ist dort ein Hansdampf in allen Gassen. Es wird nicht leicht werden, etwas so „Rückständiges" wie ein Fahrrad im Ansehen der Chinesen steigen zu lassen und so die große Verbreitung zu erhalten.

WORLDWIDE E-BIKE SALES, 2011–2015*

*2013–2015 ESTIMATED
SOURCE: ELECTRIC BIKES WORLDWIDE REPORT (EBWR) 2013

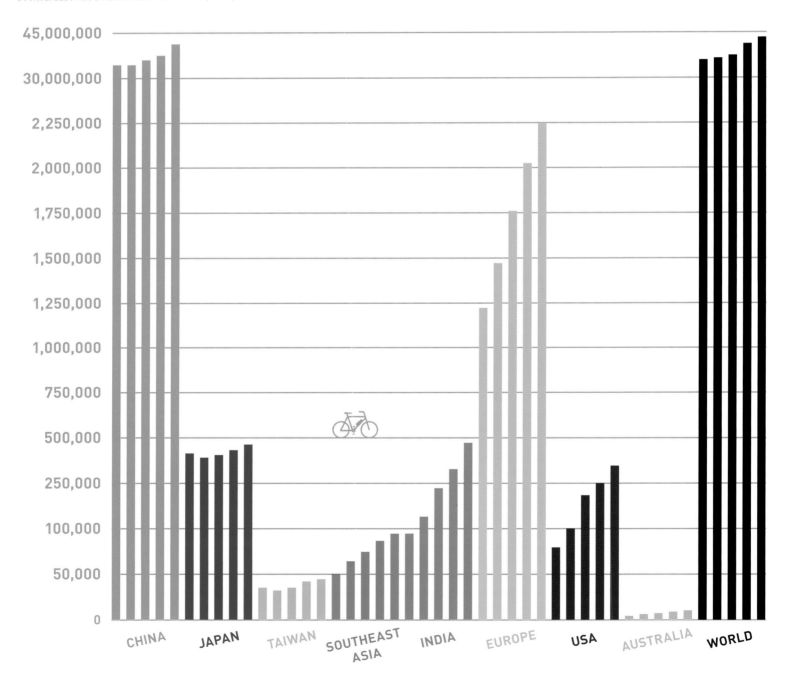

Die Herausforderung der Zukunft wird also sein, das E-Bike zum Wunschverkehrsmittel der Massen in den BRICS-Staaten (Brasilien, Russland, Indien, China und Südafrika) zu machen. Diese aufsteigenden Industrieländer müssen Lösungen für den Wunsch ihrer Bürger nach individueller Mobilität finden, ohne ihren ohnehin hohen CO_2-Ausstoß noch zu verstärken. Anders als in China fand beispielsweise in Indien die Elektromobilität lange keine Beachtung und öffentliche Busse, Taxis und Rikschas wurden statt mit Benzin mit Gas betrieben. Seit 2010 fördert die Zentralregierung gezielt die Branche und rief die „National Mission for Hybrid and Electric Vehicles" ins Leben.

Chinesische Hersteller von E-Bikes haben die Entwicklung ebenfalls erkannt und planen E-Bikes aus Europa nach China einzuführen, um so auch die Oberschicht anzusprechen. Diese darf sich heute aus Imagegründen nicht mit einem solchen Gefährt zeigen, da jeder weiß, wie kostengünstig es ist. Ähnliches galt in den 80er-Jahren in Europa, als es für Geschäftsleute verpönt war, mit dem Fahrrad zur Arbeit zu fahren. Dies hat sich erst geändert, als das Mountainbike aufkam und damit klar war, dass man aufgrund des allgemein bekannten hohen Preises eines MTB nicht aus finanziellen Gründen Fahrrad fuhr, sondern aus Gründen des gesunden Lebenswandels.

Auch für die alten Industrienationen ist der Imagewandel zum Trendfahrzeug wichtig. In Deutschland galten Fahrräder mit elektrischer Unterstützung lange als Seniorenvehikel. Dieser Ruf hängt ihnen immer noch nach. Ein wichtiger Bestandteil des Imagewandels vom Rentnerrad zum Trendbike ist die Entwicklung neuer Modelle. Sowohl das Wachstum des Marktes als auch die Produktdifferenzierung zeigen, wie das E-Bike in unterschiedlichen Zielgruppen Fuß gefasst hat. Durch neue E-Bike-Typen wie Mountainbikes, Tandems und Lastenräder werden Elektrofahrräder auch für sportliche Menschen, junge Familien und das Kleingewerbe interessant. Sicherlich wird die Generation 60plus weiter einen wichtigen Absatzmarkt darstellen, aber das Vordringen von innovativen Designs und starken Motoren kündigt eine Trendwende an.

Der Imagewandel schlägt sich auch im Preisbewusstsein nieder: Sowohl China als auch die Niederlande und Deutschland verzeichnen einen Anstieg des Durchschnittspreises für E-Bikes. Billigprodukte sind weniger gefragt, vor allem in Europa steigt die Bereitschaft, mehr als durchschnittlich 1.500 Euro für ein E-Bike auszugeben. Die Durchschnittspreise in Japan und den USA liegen umgerechnet unter 1.000 Euro.

E-BIKES & POLITICS

PROMOTING E-MOBILITY

Things are catching up on the political front as well. Tax benefits that previously applied only to company cars are now also being granted for the acquisition of e-bikes for professional purposes. This means that customers can effectively save 30% to 40% on their purchase. Politicians and traffic planners have become aware of pedelecs as the "solution" for congestion in large cities. With an improved network of bike paths and an improved charging infrastructure, e-bikes are also an attractive proposition for tourism.

Auch auf politischer Ebene wird nachgezogen. Steuerliche Vorteile, die bisher nur für Dienstwagen galten, werden jetzt auch für die berufliche Anschaffung des E-Bikes gewährt. Dies bedeutet, dass Kunden effektiv 30 bis 40 Prozent beim Kauf sparen können. Politiker und Verkehrsplaner sind auf das Pedelec als „Lösungsmittel" für verstopfte Großstädte aufmerksam geworden. E-Bikes stellen bei verbessertem Radwegenetz und verbesserter Ladeinfrastruktur außerdem einen Tourismusfaktor dar.

THE STUTTGART PEDELEC

E-BIKES: AN URBAN CASE STUDY

Stuttgart has supported e-bikes for many years. Public awareness of this support grew as a result of the 2007 pedelec race that was organized as part of the cycling world championships, which included many well-known participants including Mayor Martin Schairer. Plans are underway to further reinforce that positive feedback over the long term. This hilly city is predestined to do just that, a fact that was recognized by the city administration, which launched the Stuttgart Pedelec project and developed a unique strategy for implementing electric mobility in the city center and boosting its popularity among city residents.

Beginning in 2009, the city administration leased 20 e-bikes and had them outfitted with the official colors and the logo of the City of Stuttgart. The e-bikes are available at the town hall and at other municipal buildings. The fleet also includes 25 electric scooters that are operated in cooperation with Baden Württemberg energy provider EnBW. The Stuttgart Pedelec project is primarily aimed at City of Stuttgart employees who are frequently on the go, for example custodians who have to close up four schools every evening, or technicians who are constantly performing maintenance work. In addition, the project is intended to get people excited about a new approach to bike riding that doesn't involve sweating—particularly in a city that has differences in altitude as great as 984 feet.

Stuttgart beschäftigt sich seit Langem mit dem E-Bike. Man ist aufgrund des 2007 zur Rad-WM organisierten E-Bike-Rennens mit vielen prominenten Teilnehmern wie dem Ordnungsbürgermeister Martin Schairer auf das Thema aufmerksam geworden. Das positive Feedback soll nun langfristig verstärkt werden. Die bergige Stadt ist dafür prädestiniert, das hat auch die Stadtverwaltung erkannt, das Projekt „Stuttgart Pedelec" ins Leben gerufen und damit eine eigene Strategie entwickelt, um elektrische Mobilität in der Innenstadt zu implementieren und bei ihren Bürgern populär zu machen.

Seit 2009 hat die Stadtverwaltung 20 E-Bikes geleast und mit den offiziellen Farben und dem Logo der Stadt Stuttgart versehen. Die Elektroräder stehen im Rathaus und anderen Gebäuden der Stadtverwaltung zur Verfügung. Zur Flotte gehören zudem 25 Elektroroller, die in Kooperation mit dem baden-württembergischen Energieversorger EnBW betrieben werden. Das Projekt „Stuttgart Pedelec" richtet sich insbesondere an Angestellte der Stadt Stuttgart, die viel unterwegs sind, zum Beispiel Hausmeister, die jeden Abend vier Schulen abzuschließen haben, oder Techniker, die permanent Wartungsarbeiten durchführen. Zudem soll es die Menschen für das neue Radfahren, ohne zu schwitzen, begeistern – gerade in einer Stadt mit Höhenunterschieden von bis zu 300 Metern.

THE LANDRAD E-BIKE PROJECT

E-BIKES NOT CARS

Kairos gGmbH in the state of Vorarlberg, Austria, initiated the Landrad e-bike project in June 2008 and launched it one year later. In the largest field trial in Austria, 500 e-bikes made by Matra were sold at a discount. In return, purchasers had to provide regular reports about their riding habits. The objective of the study was to see the degree to which electric bikes could replace cars and what sort of market potential existed. Additional partners in the study included the Office of the State Government of Vorarlberg, 25 regional bicycle retailers, and the Energy Institute Vorarlberg.

Five hundred e-bikes were sold between May and July 2009. The special edition of the Matra iStep Cross pedelec sold for €1,250 ($1,630) to private parties and €1,250 plus VAT to companies and organizations. To receive this discounted price, purchasers of the "Landrad" had to agree to provide data regarding their e-bike use. To record the data, purchasers filled out online forms and returned them by e-mail. In addition, some of the e-bikes were equipped with GPS tracking systems that provided detailed information about riding behavior, range, and speed. The results will be used to help develop future projects.

One of the most important questions was whether and to what degree the e-bikes were able to replace trips by car. The survey of riders in the study showed that the e-bikes not only replaced cars but conventional bicycles as well: 52% of all trips made by e-bike would have been made using a conventional bicycle before the project and 35% with a car. Based on this data, a Landrad could save 143,000 car miles per year. In addition, one-fifth of all Landrad users reported that their mobility behavior had undergone a fundamental change because they used the Landrad far more frequently than a car. These results show that e-bikes can motivate people to leave their cars at home, an endeavor that has been less successful to date with conventional bicycles. The Swiss "E-Tour" project in 2004 showed similar results. In the E-Tour project, electric bicycles replaced 30% of all car trips, bicycle trips, and trips using public transportation. The most frequently named reasons for purchasing a Landrad underscore the persuasive power of e-bikes: "Riding a bike without sweating," "being mobile without damaging the environment," and "driving the car less."

Implemented in cooperation with commercial providers, the project demonstrates that after an initial promotion, frequently no further promotions are necessary.

Das E-Bike-Projekt „Landrad" wurde im Juni 2008 von der Kairos gGmbH im österreichischen Vorarlberg initiiert und ein Jahr später gestartet. Es ist der größte Flottenversuch in Österreich, bei dem 500 E-Bikes der Marke Matra vergünstigt abgegeben wurden. Im Gegenzug sollten die Käufer regelmäßig über ihr Fahrverhalten berichten. Ziel der Studie war es zu sehen, inwieweit das Elektrofahrrad das Auto ersetzen kann und welches Marktpotenzial besteht. Weitere Partner waren das Büro der Vorarlberger Landesregierung, 25 Fahrradhändler der Region sowie das Energieinstitut Vorarlberg.

Zwischen Mai und Juli 2009 wurden 500 E-Bikes verkauft. Der Preis der Sonderausgabe des Matra iStep Cross betrug 1.250 Euro für Privatpersonen und 1.250 Euro zuzüglich Mehrwertsteuer für Unternehmen und Organisationen. Um die Vergünstigung zu erhalten, mussten sich die Käufer des sogenannten Landrads bereit erklären, Daten über ihren Gebrauch des E-Bikes zur Verfügung zu stellen. Die Datenerfassung erfolgte über Onlineformulare, die per E-Mail zurückgesendet wurden. Zudem wurde in ausgewählten E-Bikes ein GPS-Tracking durchgeführt, um detaillierte Informationen über das Fahrverhalten, die Reichweite und die Geschwindigkeit zu erhalten. Die Ergebnisse dienen der Entwicklung zukünftiger Projekte.

Eine der wichtigsten Fragen war, ob und inwieweit das E-Bike Autofahrten ersetzen würde. Die Befragung der Testfahrer ergab, dass das E-Bike nicht nur das Auto ersetzte, sondern auch das herkömmliche Fahrrad. 52 Prozent aller mit dem E-Bike durchgeführten Wege wären vor dem Projekt mit einem gewöhnlichen Fahrrad zurückgelegt worden und 35 Prozent mit dem Auto. Mit dem Landrad konnten so schätzungsweise 230.000 Autokilometer pro Jahr eingespart werden. Zudem berichtete jeder fünfte Landrad-Benutzer, dass sich sein Mobilitätsverhalten grundlegend verändert habe, indem das Landrad wesentlich öfter verwendet wurde als das Auto. Dies zeigt, dass man Menschen mit einem E-Bike motivieren kann, ihr Auto stehen zu lassen, während dies mit einem herkömmlichen Fahrrad bisher selten gelungen ist. Ähnliche Ergebnisse lieferte 2004 das Schweizer Projekt „E-Tour". Dort ersetzten elektrische Zweiräder jeweils 30 Prozent der Autofahrten, Radfahrten und Fahrten mit öffentlichen Verkehrsmitteln. Für die Überzeugungskraft des E-Bikes sprechen auch die meistgenannten Motive für den Kauf eines Landrads: „Rad fahren, ohne zu schwitzen", „mobil sein, ohne die Umwelt zu schädigen" und „weniger Auto fahren".

Das in Zusammenarbeit mit kommerziellen Anbietern durchgeführte Projekt bezeugt, dass nach einer Initial-förderung oft keine weiteren Förderungen nötig sind.

HIGHWAYS FOR CYCLISTS ONLY

"E" STANDS FOR EXPRESS

A network of new bicycle expressways is currently being developed in the Netherlands. They are primarily aimed at persuading commuters who cover fewer than 9 miles to leave their cars at home and commute by bicycle or e-bike. Bicycle expressways sound like the dream of every cyclist: no intersections or traffic lights, smooth asphalt, and lanes that are four meters wide—plus wind protection on bridges and roofing in particularly exposed spots. The planned infrastructure of bicycle freeways also includes charging stations for electric bicycles and mobile repair services. The routes link the suburbs to city centers.

In the Netherlands, the Ministry of Infrastructure and the Environment is planning a total of 16 such expressways and has allocated a budget of $27 million to finance them. Regions and local authorities are expected to contribute another $80 million.

Speed is a crucial factor for bicycle highways, with either minimal or no waiting times at intersections or traffic lights. In addition, smooth asphalt and good lighting make the highways easy and comfortable to use. Attractive routing through natural areas and a cohesive connection to public transportation further enhance the attractiveness of the bicycle expressways.

Overall, bicycle highways make e-bikes more competitive with cars. Target groups include those who commute up to 9 miles a day, students of all ages, employees, and amateur cyclists. Riders of e-bikes are the most obvious target group, because they are frequently former car drivers, and electric bicycles offer them an alternative when normal bicycles would not be an option. Bicycle expressways are also ideal for the higher average speed of e-bikes. A study by Goudappel Coffeng shows that bicycle expressways can improve mobility, economic strength, health, and the climate. They lead to fewer trips by car, which means that as many as 80,000 tons of CO_2 emissions can be saved. Thanks to the increased physical activity, bicycle expressways can save the healthcare system $130 million. Faster bike rides can save 15,000 travel hours per day—a value equivalent to $50 million per year. Bicycle expressways additionally reduce the number of car trips by one percent, while the number of trips by bicycle increases by 1.5%.

In den Niederlanden entsteht derzeit ein Netzwerk von neuen Fahrrad-Schnellwegen. Sie sollen besonders Pendler, die weniger als 15 Kilometer zurücklegen, dazu bewegen, aus dem Auto und auf das Fahrrad oder E-Bike zu steigen. Rad-Schnellwege klingen wie der Traum eines jeden Radfahrers: keine Kreuzungen oder Ampeln, glatter Asphalt, vier Meter breite Fahrbahnen. Dazu Windschutz auf Brücken und Überdachung besonders ungeschützter Stellen. Die geplante Infrastruktur der Fahrrad-Autobahnen sieht außerdem Ladestationen für Elektrofahrräder und mobile Reparatur- services vor. Die Routen führen aus der Peripherie in die Stadtzentren.

Insgesamt 16 solcher Schnellwege sind geplant und werden mit einem Budget von 21 Millionen Euro durch das niederländische Ministerium für Infrastruktur und Umwelt finanziert. Weitere 60 Millionen Euro sollen von den Regionen und Kommunen beigesteuert werden.

Wichtigstes Kriterium für Fahrrad-Highways ist die Schnelligkeit: keine oder wenig Wartezeit an Kreuzungen oder Ampeln. Weiter- hin sorgen glatter Asphalt und Beleuchtung für eine komfortable Nutzung der Wege. Eine attraktive Routenführung durch die

GRONINGEN

AMSTERDAM

ENSCHEDE

DEN HAAG

UTRECHT

APELDOORN

ARNHEM

ROTTERDAM

'S-HERTOGENBOSCH

BREDA

EINDHOVEN

VENLO

—— ROUTE COMPLETE
—— ROUTE AT PLANNING STAGE
—— FEASIBILITY STUDY CARRIED OUT

SOURCE: WWW.FIETSFILEVRIJ.NL

Natur und eine kohärente Anbindung an den öffentlichen Personennahverkehr sichern zusätzlich die Attraktivität der Schnellwege.

Grundsätzlich verschärfen die Fahrrad-Highways die Konkurrenz zum Auto. Zielgruppen sind Pendler, die Wege bis zu 15 Kilometer zurücklegen, Schüler und Studenten, Angestellte oder schlicht Hobbyradler. E-Bike-Fahrer sind die offensichtlichste Zielgruppe, da es sich bei ihnen häufig um ehemalige Autofahrer handelt, für die ein Elektrofahrrad eine Alternative bietet, aber kein normales Rad infrage kommt. Zudem sind die Fahrrad-Schnellwege wie geschaffen für die höhere Durchschnittsgeschwindigkeit von E-Bikes. Eine Studie von Goudappel Coffeng zeigt, dass Fahrrad-Schnellwege sowohl die Mobilität, die Wirtschaftskraft, die Gesundheit als auch das Klima verbessern können. Sie führen zu weniger Autofahrten, so können bis zu 80.000 Tonnen CO_2-Emissionen eingespart werden. Durch die zusätzliche Bewegung können die Rad-Schnellwege dem Gesundheitssystem 100 Millionen Euro an Kosten ersparen. Durch schnelleres Radfahren können 15.000 Reisestunden pro Tag gespart werden, die 40 Millionen Euro im Jahr wert sind. Und durch Fahrrad-Schnellwege kann die Zahl der Autofahrten um ein Prozent reduziert und die der Radfahrten um 1,5 Prozent erhöht werden.

WHAT CAN YOU DO WITH ONE KILOWATT HOUR?

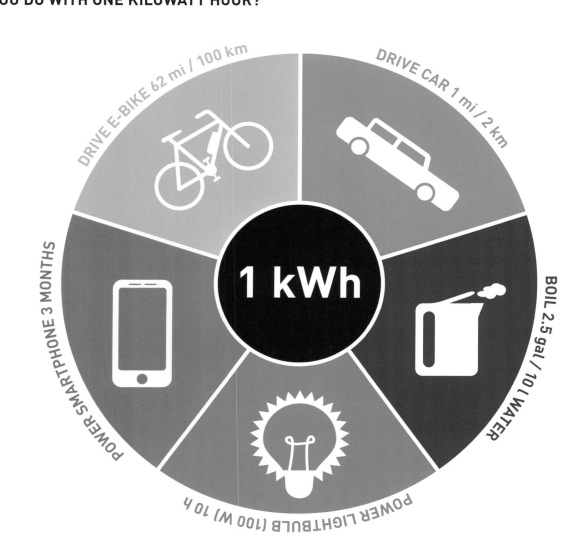

DRIVE E-BIKE 62 mi / 100 km

DRIVE CAR 1 mi / 2 km

BOIL 2.5 gal / 10 l WATER

1 kWh

POWER SMARTPHONE 3 MONTHS

POWER LIGHTBULB (100 W) 10 h

THE THREE LIVES OF A BATTERY

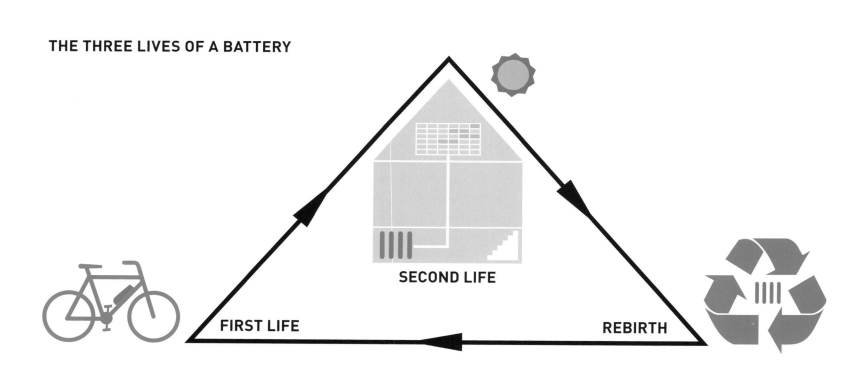

FIRST LIFE

SECOND LIFE

REBIRTH

NETWORKS
MORE EFFICIENT ENERGY SUPPLY

E-bikes can help to solve numerous environmental problems: Thanks to their electric motor, they can be operated with electricity generated from renewable energy sources such as solar, wind, and hydropower. An important cornerstone of Germany's change in energy policy is not only the switch to renewable energy sources, but also reduced energy consumption. The electric motors on e-bikes are an important component, because they have a higher efficiency level than gasoline engines. It is also more efficient to move an e-bike weighing 33 to 66 pounds than to propel an entire car weighing 1,100 to 2,200 pounds. When you consider that e-bikes replace one third of all short-distance car trips, this represents a tremendous potential. The total annual costs associated with charging an e-bike comes to only 5 to 13 dollars for a distance of 1,300 to 3,000 miles. Cyclists who ride ten miles on their e-bikes every day will only pay about 13 dollars annually to charge their e-bikes. However, this has a positive effect on the environment only if electricity from renewable energy sources is used to charge them.

Germany's change in energy policy will also affect the power supply structures: We will see a shift from a few centralized power plants to numerous small decentralized power plants. An increasing number of private households with their own photovoltaic solar systems will become part of this power grid. Unlike power plants that produce energy on a regular basis, solar and wind energy are subject to weather-related fluctuations. The challenge in this respect is to store the energy generated on good days for use on the bad days. How can e-bikes help with this undertaking? Even if the efficiency of batteries continues to increase, the capacity drops so significantly after 500 to 1,000 complete charging cycles that the batteries are no longer able to actually power an e-bike. The idea is to give batteries that are too old for e-bike use a second life as an energy storage medium. These batteries could relieve the load on the power grid: When there is surplus energy in the grid, they could store the solar electricity and, when power generation is low, they could release the stored energy. In their third life, the batteries would ultimately be recycled and new batteries would be manufactured from their components.

E-Bikes können zur Lösung zahlreicher Umweltprobleme beitragen: Durch ihren Elektromotor können sie mit Strom aus nachhaltigen Energien wie Solar-, Wind- und Wasserkraft betrieben werden. Eine wichtige Säule der Energiewende ist neben dem Umstieg auf erneuerbare Energien die Reduzierung des Energieverbrauchs. Der Elektromotor des E-Bikes ist ein wichtiger Baustein, weil er einen höheren Wirkungsgrad als ein Benzinmotor aufweist. Zudem ist es effizienter, ein E-Bike mit einem Gewicht von 15 bis 30 Kilogramm zu bewegen, als dafür ein ganzes Auto mit einem Gewicht von 500 bis 1000 Kilogramm anzutreiben. Wenn man bedenkt, dass E-Bikes ein Drittel aller Autofahrten auf Kurzstrecken ersetzen können, ist das ein großes Potenzial. Zudem kostet das Aufladen insgesamt jährlich nur vier bis zehn Euro für eine Fahrleistung von 2.000 bis 5.000 Kilometern. Wer jeden Tag 15 Kilometer auf dem E-Bike zurücklegt, zahlt für die Aufladung nur ca. zehn Euro pro Jahr. Der Umwelteffekt tritt jedoch nur dann ein, wenn die Aufladung mit Strom aus erneuerbaren Energien vorgenommen wird.

Mit der Energiewende werden sich auch die Strukturen der Stromversorgung ändern: Die Entwicklung wird vom zentralen Kraftwerk hin zu dezentralen kleinen Kraftwerken verlaufen. Auch Privathaushalte mit eigenen Solaranlagen werden vermehrt Teil dieses Stromnetzes sein. Im Gegensatz zu Kraftwerken, die regelmäßig Energieproduzieren, gibt es bei Solar- und Windenergie jedoch wetterbedingte Schwankungen. Die Herausforderung ist daher, die Energie an guten Tagen für die schlechten zu speichern. Wie können E-Bikes dazu beitragen? Auch wenn die Akkus immer effizienter werden, verringert sich die Kapazität nach 500 bis 1.000 Vollladezyklen so stark, dass sie als Antrieb für ein E-Bike ausgesorgt haben. Die Idee ist, Batterien, die zu alt für den E-Bike-Gebrauch sind, ein zweites Leben als Energiespeicher zu schenken. Die Batterien könnten das Stromnetz entlasten: Bei Überschuss im Netz könnten sie den Solarstrom zwischenspeichern, bei Strommangel im Netz die gespeicherte Energie freigeben. In ihrem dritten Leben sollen die Batterien schließlich recycelt und aus den Bestandteilen wieder neue Batterien hergestellt werden.

EVERYDAY FITNESS

VITAMIN "E"

E-bikes have benefits that extend beyond a global perspective—they also benefit the health of individuals. Who doesn't have to overcome their own inertia when it comes to exercising? E-bikes combine exercise with mobility. Commuters often have reservations about cycling because they worry about arriving at work sweaty and exhausted. E-bikes not only make exercise easy, they also make it easy to integrate activity into your daily routine. Unlike other kinds of exercise, it's a snap to get started riding an e-bike. Motor assistance helps riders who are out of shape, and riding requires little effort. Plus there are no extra expenses for equipment, including special clothing and membership fees.

With the exception of bad weather, there are no more excuses for avoiding a bit of exercise. This makes it easier for everyone to get active, including individuals who are elderly or sick, overweight, patients undergoing rehabilitation, and those returning to work, who are commonly listed as the target group for e-bikes. People with varying fitness levels can still ride and exercise together. Already there are some models that offer motor assistance based on the rider's heart rate. This feature makes it possible for people with heart conditions to exercise because the pedelec always provides additional motor assistance if the rider's pulse threatens to rise to a critical level. Achievements are documented, and miles and calories counted, all of which increases motivation and improves training. In a sense, these bikes function like mobile ergometers that can be used outdoors. E-bikes are like salad: They are healthy without being boring.

Nicht nur aus globaler Sicht haben E-Bikes Vorteile, sie tragen auch zur Gesundheit des Einzelnen bei. Wer ringt nicht mit seinem inneren Schweinehund, wenn es darum geht, Sport zu treiben. Das E-Bike verbindet Sport und Mobilität. Bei Pendlern besteht oft eine hohe Hürde, zu radeln, da sie Überanstrengung und Schwitzen noch vor Ankunft am Arbeitsplatz befürchten müssen. Mit dem E-Bike lässt sich Sport leicht und vor allem regelmäßig in den Alltag integrieren. Im Vergleich zu anderen Sportarten ist auch der Einstieg ein Kinderspiel. Schlechte Kondition kann durch die Unterstützung des Motors ausgeglichen werden, der Aufwand ist gering. Zudem fallen keine Kosten für Geräte, besondere Kleidung oder Mitgliedsbeiträge an.

Bis auf schlechtes Wetter gibt es also keine Ausflüchte mehr, sich vor ein bisschen Bewegung zu drücken. Das erleichtert den Einstieg für alle, nicht nur Ältere und Kranke, Übergewichtige, Rehapatienten und Wiedereinsteiger, die landläufig noch als die Zielgruppe für E-Bikes genannt werden. Personen mit unterschiedlicher Leistungsfähigkeit können gemeinsam fahren und trainieren. Es gibt bereits erste Modelle, die sich bei der Motorunterstützung an der Herzfrequenz orientieren. Menschen mit Herzproblemen können so wieder Sport treiben, weil das Pedelec immer dann den Motor zusteuert, wenn der Puls in einen kritischen Bereich zu steigen droht. Die Leistungen werden dokumentiert, Kilometer und Kalorien gezählt. Das motiviert und steigert den Trainingseffekt. Das Rad funktioniert quasi wie ein mobiles Ergometer, das in der Natur genutzt werden kann. E-Bikes sind wie Salat: Sie sind gesund, ohne anstrengend oder langweilig im Geschmack zu sein.

eBIKE STORY

1860

THE STEAM-POWERED BICYCLE

With the launch of the steam railroad, creative minds begin to think of ways to enhance the bicycle, also known as the "hobby horse." Pierre Michaux adds a steam engine for driving the rear wheel. As is common practice at the time, the high-wheel pedals are connected directly to the hub. Yet means of power quickly turns out to be unsuitable, since the boiler has to be heated hours ahead of time and makes the bicycle heavy and unwieldy.

Mit der Eröffnung der dampfbetriebenen Eisenbahn überlegen sich findige Köpfe, wie das Fahrrad, auch „hobby horse" genannt, verstärkt werden könnte. Pierre Michaux integriert eine Dampfmaschine, die das Hinterrad antreibt. Die Pedale des Hochrads sind, wie damals üblich, direkt mit der Nabe verbunden. Doch dieser Antrieb wird sich schnell als ungeeignet erweisen, da der Kessel schon Stunden vorher angeheizt werden muss und das Fahrrad schwer und unhandlich macht.

1885

THE FIRST RIDER

Invented by Gottlieb Daimler, the Reitwagen (riding vehicle) marks a milestone in motorcycle history. It runs on a petroleum engine and can reach a comfortable speed of 7 miles per hour. The first motorcycles with internal combustion engines go into mass production a short time later. However, the first motorcycle designs to gain acceptance are hybrids, which operate with pedals as well as with a small motor. The pedals are a safety precaution, as the motors are not yet safe or reliable. Therefore, even if the motor fails, the riders will not be stranded, but can continue on their way.

Dieser von Gottlieb Daimler erdachte Reitwagen ist ein Meilenstein in der Geschichte des Motorrads. Er wird mit einer Petroleum-Kraftmaschine betrieben und bringt es auf gemütliche 12 Kilometer pro Stunde. Kurz danach gehen auch die ersten Motorräder mit Verbrennungsmotor in Serie. Trotzdem setzen sich vorerst Hybridkonstruktionen durch, die neben einem kleinen Motor auch mit Pedalen betrieben werden können. Eine Sicherheitsmaßnahme, denn die Motoren arbeiten noch nicht sicher und zuverlässig. So bleibt man im Fall der Fälle nicht liegen und kann die Fahrt auch ohne Motor fortsetzen.

1895

THE FIRST E-BIKES

The first e-bikes are built in this year. They are used for the extremely popular motorsport called pacemaker racing, in which a pacemaker rides ahead of the actual athletes and clears the way. These races cover long distances and are ridden at a consistently high speed. To keep ahead, the pacemaker must have power assistance. Around 20 electric racing teams participate in the race. But as the safety and reliability of internal combustion engines increase, the e-bikes vanish from the track.

Die ersten E-Bikes werden in diesem Jahr gebaut. Sie werden für die sehr beliebten Schrittmacher-Rennen einge-setzt, eine Radsportart, bei der vor dem eigentlichen Sportler ein Schrittmacher fährt und für Windschatten sorgt. Diese Rennen finden auf langen Distanzen bei hoher, konstanter Geschwindigkeit statt. Um mitzuhalten, ist für den Schrittmacher eine Energiehilfe unerlässlich. Etwa 20 solcher elektrischen Rennteams mischen bei den Rennen mit. Doch mit der wachsenden Zuverlässigkeit und Sicherheit von Verbrennungsmotoren verschwinden die E-Bikes wieder von der Piste.

1860

1885

1895

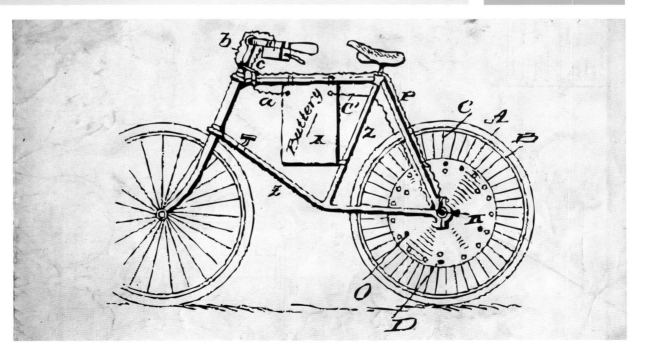

1932

N.V. SIMPLEX

1952

NO NEED TO PEDAL NOW !

Over 50,000 cyclists in this country have motorised their bicycles with Cyclemaster, the engine-in-a-wheel which replaces the rear wheel of your own machine. Centre of gravity is lowered, making the cycle safer to ride. Positive chain drive eliminates slip in wet weather. Luggage carrier and front forks left unencumbered. Travel when and where you like without fatigue. 20 m.p.h. 250 m.p.g.

KYR 347

£27 . 10 . 0

including special wheel and tyre and safety back-pedalling hub brake.

Cyclemaster

1975

1932

THE FIRST MASS-PRODUCED MODEL

EMI, a Philips subsidiary, introduces the first mass-market bicycle with an electric auxiliary drive in 1932. This bike is remarkably similar to today's models. Its motor is positioned low down for good weight distribution, a charger feeds power to the glass battery, and the e-bike even has a motor controller. However, there are problems with the power regulation, since power electronics are not yet available. At the same time, researchers in London study a hub motor mounted on the rear wheel, which also provides a regeneration function (recovering energy from the brakes).

EMI, eine Tochterfirma von Philips, stellt 1932 das erste serienmäßige Fahrrad mit elektrischem Zusatzantrieb vor. Dieses Rad weist erstaunliche Ähnlichkeiten mit den heutigen Modellen auf: Der Motor sitzt tief für eine gute Gewichtsverteilung, die Batterie aus Glas wird über ein Ladegerät gespeist und eine Motorbedienung gibt es auch schon. Allerdings ist die Kraftdosierung mit Schwierigkeiten verbunden, da es noch keine Leistungselektronik gibt. In London wird zur selben Zeit an einem Nabenmotor im Hinterrad geforscht, der auch Rekuperation (Wieder-gewinnung von Bremsenergie) vorsieht.

1952

THE POST-WAR ERA

"No need to pedal now": This slogan from an ad for a motorized bicycle perfectly expresses the spirit of the times. The war destroyed Germany's infrastructure, and no one has much money. "Stottervelos," bikes with a small internal combustion engine, become popular. Often, a one- or two-cylinder motor is simply mounted on a bicycle. However, they are only a stop-gap solution, as the car with its potential for unlimited mobility becomes an increasingly sought-after status symbol.

„Warum treten, wenn es auch ohne geht" – das ist der Werbeslogan für ein motorisiertes Zweirad und bringt den Zeitgeist gut auf den Punkt. Der Krieg hat die Infrastruktur zerstört und die Menschen haben wenig Geld. „Stotter-velos", Räder mit kleinem Verbrennungshilfsmotor, werden beliebt. Oft werden vorhandene Fahrräder einfach mit einem Ein- oder Zweizylinder nachgerüstet. Doch sie bleiben eine Übergangslösung – das Auto wird zum Status-symbol und unbedingten Mobilitätsversprechen.

1975

REDISCOVERING THE BICYCLE

Konosuke Matsushita, who founded Panasonic, is considered one of the most important entrepreneurs of the 20th century. In the early 1970s, he introduced an e-bike that closely resembles today's models. As the oil crisis sets in, people begin to return to their bicycles and e-bikes. The development of mountain bikes also helps change the bicycle's image, so that it is no longer just for kids anymore, but becomes a coveted piece of leisure sports equipment.

Konosuke Matsushita, der Firmengründer von Panasonic, gilt als einer der bedeutendsten Unternehmer des 20. Jahrhunderts. Anfang der 70er stellt er ein E-Bike vor, das den heutigen Modellen sehr ähnelt. Mit Ausbruch der Ölkrise wird die Abhängigkeit von Benzin augenfällig. Infolgedessen erinnert man sich wieder an Fahrräder und „E-Bikes". Die Entwicklung von Mountainbikes bewirkt zusätzlich einen Imagewechsel für das Fahrrad: weg vom Kinderspielzeug, hin zum begehrenswerten Freizeitsportgerät.

1989

THE TRAVELING VACUUM CLEANER

A nickel cadmium battery that is driven by a hub motor based on a vacuum cleaner motor is an integral part of the mass-market Sanyo Enacle bike. The same year, the German manufacturer Hercules tests its Electra model. Along with these pioneering projects comes the question of how fast e-bikes should be allowed to go before their owners must attach insurance stickers and wear a helmet. Power assist technology catches on in Japan. Under a new law, motor power may be applied only in proportion to muscle power.

Bei dem Sanyo Enacle wird serienmäßig ein Nickel-Cadmium-Akku eingebaut, der von einem Nabenmotor betrieben wird. Dieser basiert auf einem Staubsaugermotor. Im selben Jahr erprobt der deutsche Hersteller Hercules sein Modell Electra. Beide Pionierprojekte begleitet die Frage, wie schnell E-Bikes sein dürfen, ohne dass Versicherungs-kennzeichen und Helm verbindlich werden. So setzt sich die Power-Assist-Technik in Japan durch. Es wird gesetzlich festgelegt, dass der Motor nicht stärker als die Muskelkraft sein darf.

1994

EQUAL RIGHTS FOR EVERYONE

In 1994, thanks to targeted lobbying by Yamaha, the Japanese power assist system, which makes the pedelec legally equivalent to a bicycle, is recognized by German law. Shortly thereafter, regulation is harmonized throughout Europe. The first pedelec to be manufactured in Europe is the Yoker, introduced by ITG Zschopau. It is built in the former MZ motorcycle plant with support from Egon Gelhard, who had patented the pedelec principle back in 1982.

Durch die gezielte Lobbyarbeit von Yamaha wird das Power-Assist-System aus Japan, welches das Pedelec dem Fahrrad juristisch gleichsetzt, 1994 auch in Deutschland ins Gesetzbuch übernommen. Kurz darauf gilt die Regelung europaweit. Als erstes Pedelec aus europäischer Produktion präsentiert ITG Zschopau den Yoker. Er entsteht in den ehemaligen MZ Motorradwerken mit Unterstützung von Egon Gelhard, der sich das Pedelec-Prinzip schon 1982 hat patentieren lassen.

1999

BREAKTHROUGH IN CHINA

In the late 1990s, China takes political action that helps build its electric bicycle industry from the ground up to become the market leader. To fight air pollution, e-bikes receive tax incentives that favor them over two-stroke motorcycles. However, all two-wheelers are classified as electric bicycles as long as they only have pedal stumps or pedal-crank bearings. Moreover, poor recycling practices often introduce lead sludge and acid into the environ-ment. At the same time, European manufacturers are looking for new frame and battery materials. The Yellow Dream racing bike from La Prima, for example, has a frame made of hardened carbon fiber.

Ende der 90er-Jahre wird China durch politische Maßnahmen aus dem Nichts zum Marktführer für elektrische Zweiräder. Um die Luftverschmutzung zu vermindern, werden diese gegenüber Zweitaktmotorrädern steuerlich begünstigt. Dem Gesetz zufolge gelten allerdings alle Zweiräder als Elektrofahrrad, solange sie nur Pedalstummel oder Tretlager besitzen. Häufig gelangen außerdem durch unzureichendes Recycling Bleischlamm und Säure in die Umwelt. Gleichzeitig wird in Europa nach neuen Materialien für Rahmen und Akkus gesucht. Der Rahmen des Rennrads Yellow Dream von La Prima wird beispielsweise aus gefestigter Kohlefaser hergestellt.

1989

各部の名称

ENACLE エナクル

バックミラー
キーボックス
アクセルグリップ
バッテリー
（ニカド電池内蔵）
前照灯
番号灯
書類ケース
ブレーキスイッチ
駆動部

CY-B1（N）ゴールド

1994

Yoker

1999

塑造城市精神

网址 w.11yh-sh.com

24H 全年无休

2002

2010

2012

2002

LITHIUM BATTERY INTRODUCED

The old lead batteries are replaced by lighter-weight and more powerful lithium batteries. This technology accelerates e-bike development, since the batteries have a longer range and increase safety. The smaller batteries are also lighter weight and can be integrated less conspicuously into the frame design. In just ten years after the introduction of lithium technology, the capacity of the lithium battery has nearly quadrupled, without adding to its size or weight.

Die alte Bleibatterie wird durch leichtere und leistungsfähigere Lithiumakkus ersetzt. Dies beflügelt die Entwicklung der E-Bikes, da die Akkus eine höhere Reichweite besitzen und die Sicherheit erhöhen. Zudem lassen sich die kleineren Batterien leichter und unauffälliger ins Rahmendesign integrieren. In nur zehn Jahren seit der Einführung der Lithiumtechnologie hat sich deren Kapazität bei gleicher Größe und gleichem Gewicht fast vervierfacht.

2010/2011

NETWORK EXPANSION

Market forecasts predict rapid growth in the electrically powered sector. In 2010, Bosch begins to ship electric drives, and 13 auto manufacturers are quick to follow the new trend. In January 2011, production in Normandy increases to a capacity of 300,000 bikes per year. Bike sharing and rental systems grow along with the commercialization of the technology. Peugeot launches its Mu rental service in 2011. Bicycles, pedelecs, electric scooters and e-cars become available for rent in central locations in Milan and Rome.

Marktprognosen sagen ein großes Wachstum im Elektroantriebsgeschäft voraus. Bosch beginnt 2010 Elektroantriebe zu liefern und 13 Fahrradhersteller springen auf den neuen Trend auf. Im Januar 2011 wird die Produktion in der Normandie auf eine Kapazität von 300.000 Stück pro Jahr ausgebaut. Parallel zur Kommerzialisierung der Technik entwickeln sich Share- und Mietsysteme. Der Autohersteller Peugeot startet 2011 seinen Mietservice Mu. In Mailand und Rom werden an zentralen Orten Fahrräder, Pedelecs, Elektroroller und E-Autos verliehen.

2012

CHARGING AHEAD

On successfully completing market tests, and after the International Electrotechnical Commission (IEC) adopts the EnergyBus Protocol for light electric vehicles, the EnergyBus power plug is approved in March 2012, paving the way for a standardized charging infrastructure.

Nach erfolgreichem Markttest und einer Einigung der International Electrotechnical Commission (IEC) auf das EnergyBus-Protokoll für den Bereich der Leicht-Elektrofahrzeuge wird im März 2012 der EnergyBus-Stecker freigegeben. Damit ist der Weg zu einer einheitlichen Ladeinfrastruktur geebnet.

TECHNOLOGY

ANATOMY OF A BIKE

TERMINOLOGY BABBLE

||||||||||||||||||||||||||||||||||||||||||||||||||||||||||||||||||||||||||||||||

All e-bikes are not created equal. The technical designations and legal classifications vary from one country to another. A wide range exists which vary in terms of their maximum assisted speed, type of drive, and motor power.

In Germany, for example, electric bikes are classified as LEVs (light electric vehicles) and are available in two main types: Pedelec 25 and Pedelec 45. There are also a number of unusual bike models that have much in common with electric scooters.

The classic electric bicycles are known as pedelecs (PEDal ELEctric Cycles) and account for 90 percent of all LEVs sold in the leading European markets (Germany and the Netherlands). They also make up the largest group of bikes discussed in this book. E-bikes are by definition self-powered electric bicycles—motor vehicles that require proof of insurance. However, bikes that come under this definition are sold almost exclusively in China and are not relevant to the European market. In this book, we therefore use the terms e-bike and pedelec interchangeably. It would be wrong to think of these bikes as vehicles for senior citizens. Despite having motors, they are designed for athletes and people who enjoy exercise. The exercise-averse would do better to buy a moped, since the Pedelec 25's motor provides assistance only while the rider is pedaling. Speed demons will also find little satisfaction in a Pedelec 25, since the motor provides no assistance at speeds above 15 miles per hour (20 miles per hour in the United States). To go faster, riders need to apply their own muscle power. The trade-off for this limitation is that the law treats Pedelec 25 bikes just like normal bicycles and does not require a helmet, driver's license, or proof of insurance.

To reach higher speeds without physical exertion, you can upgrade to a Pedelec 45. The number 45 stands for the maximum assisted speed (in kilometers) that this model allows while the rider is pedaling. Traveling at these speeds usually means riding alongside cars and not on normal bike paths. However, these bikers need to comply with certain insurance, sticker, and helmet laws, depending on the legislation regarding motor power and speed applicable in their home country.

The E-Bike 45 models begin with speedsters that have very little in common with bicycles apart from their pedals; yet these are still considered e-bikes. They are subject to the same regulations as vehicles such as electric scooters that are approved for speeds of 28 miles per hour, which once again blurs the distinction between a scooter and an E-Bike 45, whose pedals are not really that important—if there are any at all.

E-Bike ist nicht gleich E-Bike. In jedem Land sind die Bezeichnungen für die Technik und die juristische Klassifizierung unterschiedlich. Es gibt eine Vielzahl von Modellen, die sich in maximaler Unterstützungsgeschwindigkeit, Antriebsart und Motorenleistung voneinander unterscheiden.

In Deutschland unterteilt man beispielsweise Elektrofahrräder unter dem Oberbegriff „LEV" (Leicht-Elektro-Vehikel) hauptsächlich nach Pedelecs 25 und Pedelecs 45, dazu kommen einige seltene Bike-Modelle, bei denen die Grenze zu Elektrorollern und Scootern fließend sein kann.

Pedelecs (PEDal ELEctric Cycles) gelten als die klassischen Elektrofahrräder – sie machen 90 Prozent aller verkauften LEV in den europäischen Leitmärkten Deutschland und den Niederlanden aus und stellen auch die größte Gruppe der im Buch gezeigten Bikes dar. E-Bikes sind von der Definition her selbstfahrende Elektrofahrräder und damit versicherungspflichtige Kraftfahrzeuge. Bikes nach dieser Definition werden allerdings fast ausschließlich in China verkauft, sie sind in Europa nicht marktrelevant. In diesem Buch wird der Begriff E-Bike daher als Synonym für Pedelec verwendet. Wer diese Räder für ein Seniorenvehikel hält, liegt falsch – trotz des Motors sind sie für Sportskanonen und Menschen, die Freude an Bewegung haben, gemacht. Faulpelze sollten sich lieber ein Mofa zulegen, denn auf Pedelecs 25 hilft der Motor nur dann mit, wenn tatsächlich in die Pedale getreten wird. Das

Fahrrad kann daher nicht wie ein Motorrad genutzt werden. Auch Raser werden mit einem Pedelec 25 nicht glück-lich werden, denn ab einer Geschwindigkeit von 25 Kilometern pro Stunde (in den USA 32 Kilometern pro Stunde) beendet der Motor die Unterstützung. Wer schneller fahren möchte, muss ab dieser Geschwindigkeit mit seiner eigenen Muskelkraft aufstocken. Der Vorteil dieser Beschränkungen ist, dass Pedelecs 25 gesetzlich wie normale Fahrräder behandelt werden und weder Helm-, Führerschein- noch Versicherungspflicht besteht.

Wer es ohne körperliche Anstrengung noch schneller wünscht, kann auf Pedelecs 45 umsteigen. Die 45 steht für die zulässige maximale Unterstützungsgeschwindigkeit dieser Spezies bei Mittreten des Fahrers. Wer so schnell unterwegs ist, muss meistens auch auf der Straße fahren und darf nicht die normalen Radwege nutzen. Je nach Motorleistung, Geschwindigkeit, Land und Gesetzeslage müssen allerdings bestimmte Auflagen zur Versicherung, Kennzeichen-Anbringung oder Helmpflicht beachtet werden.

Danach beginnt die Welt der E-Bikes 45 mit schnellen Krachern, die mit Fahrrädern außer den Pedalen nicht mehr ganz so viel gemeinsam haben, aber trotzdem noch E-Bikes sind. Für sie gelten die gleichen Bestimmungen wie beispielsweise einen Motorroller, der bis 45 Kilometer pro Stunde zugelassen ist – und hier verschwimmen dann auch leicht die Grenzen zu einem E-Bike 45, bei dem die Pedale schnell in den Hintergrund treten, falls sie über-haupt noch vorhanden sind.

PEDELEC 25

→ Pedal assistance up to 15 mph

→ Legal requirements are the same as for a bicycle

→ No proof of insurance/driver's license/ helmet required

→ Tretunterstützung bis 25 km/h

→ gesetzlich dem Fahrrad gleichgestellt

→ keine Versicherungs- / Führerschein- / Helmpflicht

PEDELEC 45

→ Pedal assistance up to 28 mph

→ Completely electrically powered up to 12 mph by means of a hand control

→ Insurance sticker required/moped license/ helmet required (bicycle helmet)

→ Tretunterstützung bis 45 km/h

→ fährt per Handbedienung bis 20 km/h auch rein elektrisch

→ Versicherungskennzeichen-Pflicht / Mofa- Prüfbescheinigung / Helmpflicht (Fahrradhelm)

E-BIKE 45

→ Pedal power not required for operation

→ Can be completely electrically powered up to 28 mph by means of a hand control

→ Insurance sticker required/Class M driver's license/helmet required (motorcycle helmet)

→ funktioniert auch ohne Pedalkraft

→ fährt per Handbedienung bis 45 km/h rein elektrisch

→ Versicherungskennzeichen-Pflicht / Führerschein Klasse M / Helmpflicht (Motorradhelm)

THE MOTOR
AT THE HEART OF THE MATTER

A classic e-bike has a drive consisting of multiple components. At its heart is the electric motor, which, as in a car, can be placed in various locations: in front, in the middle, or on the rear wheel. When designed as a hub motor, it drives either the front or rear wheel, while a center motor is mounted near the pedal-crank bearing. There is no general consensus on the best placement for the motor; it all depends on the bike's intended use.

The center motor is the most common type. This extremely robust motor ensures good weight distribution. Riders can easily fix flat tires, since the electric components are located in the vehicle frame and not on the wheels. As a result, center motors are usually not suitable for retrofitting normal bicycles.

Another option is to mount a hub motor on the rear wheel. However, this arrangement complicates changing a flat tire and makes the entire bicycle very tail-heavy, especially if the battery is mounted near the rear rack and luggage is also piled on top. A hub motor can also be mounted on the front wheel. The advantage of this arrangement is that it permits normal operation of the coaster brake, which is not always possible with center and rear wheel motors. This variant is a dual-drive vehicle and therefore also especially easy to ride. Pedaling drives the rear wheel, while the motor powers the front wheel. However, there are a few pitfalls as well: The handlebars tend to swerve more rapidly on a hill or if the road surface is wet. Some of the less common specialty bikes also come with all-wheel drives.

Add-on kits for the front or rear wheel can be purchased for retrofitting a bicycle with a motor. But if you plan to retrofit your own bike, be aware that the frame of a normal bicycle is not always designed for the added forces and the brakes must also tolerate the faster speeds. Moreover, the question of insurance coverage is a gray area, since the extent of the manufacturer's liability is no longer clear. Experts therefore advise against retrofitting your own bicycle.

Pedelec 25 motors usually have a continuous power rating of 250 watts. A 500-watt continuous power rating is also permitted for Pedelec 45 models. The United States allows a 500-watt continuous power rating for all pedelecs

and e-bikes, while some e-bikes can even exceed 2,000 watts. The indicated power ratings and peak power output actually achieved can vary enormously. This is due to the electric motor's general maximum load tolerance as well as to the fact that many manufacturers build motors that are simply much more powerful. However, they have an electronic throttle to meet legal requirements and also achieve higher efficiency ratings when riding the e-bike over mountainous terrain.

Der Antrieb eines klassischen E-Bikes besteht aus mehreren Komponenten. Das Herzstück ist der Elektromotor, der, ähnlich wie bei Autos, an verschiedenen Stellen vorne, mittig oder hinten am Rad platziert sein kann. Entweder treibt er als Nabenmotor das Vorder- oder Hinterrad an oder er ist als Mittelmotor im Bereich des Tretlagers angebracht. Die Frage nach der optimalen Platzierung ist nicht eindeutig zu beantworten und hängt vom Einsatzgebiet des Bikes ab.

Am gängigsten ist der Mittelmotor, der für eine gute Gewichtsverteilung sorgt und als sehr robust gilt. Reifenpannen können einfach behoben werden, da die Technik im Fahrradrahmen und nicht an den Rädern steckt. Daher sind Mittelmotoren in der Regel auch nicht nachträglich an normalen Rädern montierbar.

Eine andere Variante ist der Nabenmotor im Hinterrad. Allerdings ist bei einer Panne der Radwechsel kompliziert und das gesamte Gefährt wird sehr hecklastig, vor allem wenn die Batterie im Bereich des Gepäckträgers untergebracht ist und dieser dann auch noch beladen wird. Eine weitere Option ist ein Nabenmotor im Vorderrad. Dieser hat den Vorteil, dass die Rücktrittbremse normal bedient werden kann – das ist bei Mittel- und Hinterradmotoren nicht immer der Fall. Darüber hinaus lässt sich diese Variante besonders leicht fahren, da es sich um ein Gefährt mit Doppelantrieb handelt: Durch das Treten der Pedale wird das Hinterrad angetrieben, durch den Motor das Vorderrad. Aber auch hier lauern Tücken: Der Lenker kann am Berg oder bei Nässe schneller ins Schlingern geraten. Einige seltene Spezialvarianten ermöglichen auch Allradantrieb.

Wer sein Fahrrad mit einem Motor nachrüsten möchte, kann Zusatz-Kits für das Vorder- oder Hinterrad kaufen. Aber bei der Selbstmontage ist Vorsicht geboten: Nicht immer ist der Rahmen eines normalen Fahrrads auf die neu einwirkenden Kräfte ausgelegt, auch die Bremsen müssen die Geschwindigkeit aushalten können. Zudem bewegt man sich versicherungstechnisch schnell in einer Grauzone, da die Herstellerhaftung nicht mehr eindeutig geklärt werden kann. Experten raten daher von der Selbstmontage ab.

Pedelec-25-Motoren haben in der Regel eine Dauer-Nennleistung von 250 Watt. Bei Pedelecs 45 ist eine 500-Watt-Dauer-Nennleistung erlaubt. In den USA ist bei allen Pedelecs und E-Bikes eine 500-Watt-Dauer-Nennleistung zugelassen. Einige E-Bikes kommen sogar auf über 2000 Watt. Die angegebenen Leistungen und die tatsächlichen Spitzenleistungen klaffen oft weit auseinander. Dies liegt zum einen an der generellen Spitzenlastfähigkeit von Elektromotoren und zum anderen daran, dass viele Hersteller Motoren verbauen, die prinzipiell wesentlich mehr leisten könnten. Allerdings sind diese elektronisch gedrosselt, um einerseits die gesetzlichen Vorgaben zu erfüllen und andererseits höhere Wirkungsgrade auch bei Bergfahrten zu realisieren.

SENSORS, TRANSMISSIONS, DISPLAYS

THE BRAIN

E-bikes are hybrid vehicles. While hybrid cars feature two types of drives, such as a natural gas or gasoline engine and an electric motor, hybrid bikes combine muscle power with an electric drive. A special sensor is built into the bike to maintain an ideal ratio between these two forces when they are being applied simultaneously. This sensor sends an activation signal to the motor when required. In most cases, two types of sensors are used in combination.

The motion sensor determines whether the pedals are in operation. If they are, the motor automatically accelerates to a preset speed limit—9 miles per hour, for example. Pedaling therefore activates an on/off switching function, and the bike can be ridden much like an electric scooter. However, experts take a skeptical view of this technology, arguing that bikes with motion sensors are not true hybrid vehicles because they can also be ridden without muscle power. The term "bicycle" is a misnomer in this case, and they are more properly classified as motor vehicles.

The supplementary function of the force sensor, which is also known as a torque sensor, works differently. This sensor not only determines whether the rider is pedaling but also how fast, and it supplies power in proportion to the muscle power—the more strenuous the ride, the more power the motor provides. Various measurement techniques are used. Some sensors measure the flexural load on a component that bends only slightly under the application of muscle power. The wheel axle, pedal-crank bearing axle, and the right, rear dropout of the bicycle frame are particularly suitable for this purpose. Ideally, the measurement should include multiple factors in order to supply the proper amount of energy. In a good e-bike, muscle and motor power work together in harmony and ensure intuitive operation.

Automation is also making inroads into gear-shift systems. Modern e-bikes often come with more than eight speeds, combined with other power assist modes. This means that shifting can become quite complicated. Incorrect settings reduce motor efficiency, and the range and shifting of the derailleur under pressure can cause the chain to wear out quickly. Based on the planetary gear invented by Leonardo da Vinci in 1490, some models therefore also have a built-in, stepless automatic transmission that improves the interaction between the transmission, motor,

drive train. Approaches that push the limits of mechanical transmissions and vary the transition electronically deserve special mention. In electronic bikes, for example, the chain is completely replaced by an electric cable, and a pedal-powered generator takes up the muscle power. In this way the pedal power and frequency can therefore be fully optimized to the rider's needs. However, this approach is still very difficult to implement.

Most e-bikes have displays that range from simple menus with two buttons (on/off and mode selection) to complex functional displays. The most important function is the battery charge level indicator. You can often select different power assist settings such as "Sports" or "Tour" on the display. Most e-bikes have three settings: "Eco" for normal biking with economical power assistance; "Sports," a mode that provides short-term, intensive assistance but consumes high amounts of power; and "Tour," which is ideal for longer rides and is light on the batteries. Other functions include a speedometer, which displays the speed and miles traveled, the distance remaining, and other statistical data, such as the average speed. Technical feedback about the bike, such as a light indicator, can also be transmitted. On some bikes, the display can operate as a key, so that removing the display from the bike immobilizes the motor.

New technologies are moving toward smartphone integration. Usually placed on the handlebars, the smartphone offers the potential to add new apps for special functions, such as planning routes, navigation, tracking the bike via GPS, displaying nearby charging stations, and networking with car-sharing services such as Car2go. Some bike models are designed specifically for rehab training and offer a function for matching the heart rate with an appropriate motor power, so that the rider can train without the risk of overexertion, and so that the bike is correctly programmed for further use.

A possible future scenario could look like this: Pedestrians and bikers have an app on their smartphones that automatically communicates with car navigation systems and tachometers. The static traffic divisions on the road are removed, being replaced by digital sidewalks and bike paths that adapt to the traffic and its users. In residential areas, the lighter vehicles automatically get the right of way, and cars brake automatically or yield when a pedestrian or bike crosses their lane. Pedestrians receive a warning of potential collisions on their smartphones. This may sound like science fiction from today's perspective, but such scenarios involve little more than linking existing technologies.

E-Bikes sind Hybridfahrzeuge. Während beim Automobil ein Hybrid das Vorhandensein von zwei Antriebsarten wie Gas-, Benzin- oder Elektromotor bezeichnet, bedeutet Hybridbike die Kombination von Muskelkraft und Elektromotor. Um diese Kräfte bei gleichzeitiger Nutzung in ein ideales Verhältnis zu setzen, ist ein spezieller Sensor in die Bikes eingebaut. Dieser sendet dem Motor ein Signal, wenn er sich einschalten soll. Meist kommen dabei zwei Sensorenarten zum Einsatz.

Der Bewegungssensor misst, ob in die Pedale getreten wird oder nicht. Dann beschleunigt der Motor automatisch auf eine voreingestellte Endgeschwindigkeit, zum Beispiel 15 Kilometer pro Stunde. Das Treten funktioniert also wie ein An- und Ausschalter und das Bike kann nach dem Prinzip eines Motorrollers genutzt werden. Diese Technik wird in der Fachwelt allerdings kritisch beurteilt. Der Vorwurf: Bikes mit Bewegungssensor sind keine echten Hybridfahrzeuge, weil man auch ohne Muskelkraft fahren kann. Sie haben den Status „Fahrrad" zu Unrecht inne und zählen eher zu der Gruppe der Kraftfahrzeuge.

Anders arbeitet das additive Verfahren des Kraftsensors, alternativ auch als Drehmomentsensor bezeichnet. Dieser misst nicht nur, ob, sondern auch, wie stark in die Pedale getreten wird, und schaltet die Energie proportional zur Muskelkraft zu – je anstrengender die Fahrt, desto mehr hilft der Motor. Es werden verschiedene Techniken zum Messen eingesetzt: Manche Sensoren messen die Biegebelastung auf einem Bauteil, welches sich durch die Muskelkraft minimal verbiegt. Besonders eignen sich dazu die Radachse, die Tretlagerachse oder auch das rechte hintere Ausfallende des Fahrradrahmens. Idealerweise fließen mehrere Faktoren bei der Messung ein, um möglichst sinnvoll Energie dazuzuschalten. Bei einem guten E-Bike arbeiten Muskel- und Motorkraft harmonisch zusammen und machen es intuitiv bedienbar.

Auch bei den Gangschaltungssystemen gibt es Tendenzen zur Automatisierung. Moderne E-Bikes sind häufig mit mehr als acht Gängen ausgestattet, kombiniert mit weiteren Unterstützungsmodi des Motors. Das Schalten kann daher schnell zu einer komplexen Angelegenheit werden. Falsche Einstellungen verringern den Wirkungsgrad des Motors sowie die Reichweite und das Schalten einer Kettenschaltung unter Last führt zum schnellen Verschleiß der Kette. Basierend auf dem 1490 von Leonardo da Vinci erfundenen Planetengetriebe, ist bei einigen Modellen daher auch eine stufenlose Automatikschaltung eingebaut, die das Zusammenspiel von Schaltung, Motor und Muskelkraft verbessert. Einige Hersteller arbeiten an der Integration der Muskelkraft-Schaltung in den elektrischen Antriebsstrang. Besonders erwähnenswert sind Ansätze, die Grenzen der mechanischen Schaltung zu sprengen und elektronisch die Übersetzung zu variieren – beim sogenannten „electronic bike" ist die Kette durch

ein elektrisches Kabel gänzlich ersetzt und die Muskelkraft wird über einen Tretgenerator aufgenommen. So können Trittleistung und Frequenz ganz auf die Bedürfnisse des Fahrers optimiert werden. Noch ist dies jedoch sehr schwierig in der Umsetzung.

E-Bikes verfügen in der Regel über Displays, welche von einfachen Menüs mit zwei Knöpfen (An/Aus und Moduswahl) bis hin zum Aufzeigen komplexer Funktionen variieren. Die wichtigste Funktion ist die Anzeige der Akkurestdauer. Über das Display können oft die verschiedenen Unterstützungseinstellungen wie „Sport" oder „Tour" gewählt werden. Die meisten E-Bikes bieten drei Einstellungen an: „Eco" für normales Fahren mit ökonomischer Unterstützung, „Sport", ein Modus, der eher kurzfristig und intensiv, aber mit hohem Verbrauch unterstützt, oder „Tour", der für größere Ausflüge mit langer Akkudauer ideal ist. Hinzu kommen Tachofunktionen, die Geschwindigkeit und gefahrene Kilometer, Restdistanz und weitere statistische Daten wie zum Beispiel die Durchschnittsgeschwindigkeit anzeigen. Auch technische Rückmeldungen über das Rad wie eine Lichtanzeige können übermittelt werden. Bei einigen Bikes kann das Display als Schlüssel fungieren, sodass mit Abnahme des Displays vom Rad eine Wegfahrsperre aktiviert wird.

Die technische Entwicklung geht hin zur Smartphone-Integration. Das meist auf dem Lenker platzierte Smartphone eröffnet über spezielle Apps weitere Möglichkeiten wie Routenplanung, Navigation, GPS-Tracking des Bikes, die Anzeige von Ladestationen in der Nähe und die Vernetzung mit Carsharing-Services wie zum Beispiel Car2go. Einige Modelle sind speziell auf den Reha-Betrieb ausgelegt und verbinden die Herzratenmessung mit einer angemessenen Motorleistung, um die Grenze zwischen Training und Überanstrengung nicht zu überschreiten und das Bike für den weiteren Gebrauch richtig einzustellen.

Ein mögliches Zukunftsszenario könnte so aussehen: Über eine App kommunizieren die Smartphones der Fußgänger und Fahrradfahrer automatisch mit den Navigationssystemen und Tachometern der Autos. Die Einteilung der Straße wird aufgehoben und es entstehen digitale Bürgersteige und Fahrradwege, die sich an den Verkehr und seine Teilnehmer anpassen. In Wohngebieten bekommen die jeweils schwächeren Verkehrsteilnehmer automatisch Vorfahrt und die Autos bremsen automatisch ab oder weichen aus, wenn ein Fußgänger oder Radfahrer ihre Fahrbahn kreuzt. Fußgänger werden über ihre Smartphones vor einer potenziellen Kollision gewarnt. Das klingt heute futuristisch, ist aber kaum mehr als die Verknüpfung bereits vorhandener Technik.

THE BATTERY

THE DELICATE ORGAN

The motor is driven by a battery that the user can remove from the bicycle and charge with a charger connected to any wall outlet. The means of the battery's attachment to the bicycle varies, depending on the design and brand. Some manufacturers suspend the batteries below the rear rack, while others hide them in the frame. In some models, they are camouflaged as water bottles or saddlebags.

Modern batteries use lithium-based electrochemical elements as the anode material and usually weigh between two and seven pounds. Batteries must be recharged an average of every 30 miles; the range fluctuates, depending on the road conditions, the rider's weight, and the power-assist mode used.

Some models with gearless hub motors have electric brakes that convert the braking power back into electric energy, thereby slightly recharging the battery. With today's technology, the use of such "regeneration" usually extends the range by 8 to 15 percent. One vision of the future uses the principle of energy recovery while riding the bike, which includes disconnecting the muscle power when the biker is pedaling efficiently and recovering the stored energy when the user's efficiency is poor. Although this technology is still in the early stages, the first functional prototype, the Bike+, already exists (see chapter "Products," p 202).

Batteries have key figures that indicate the battery energy level and performance. As a rule, manufacturers state these values in volts (V), ampere-hours (Ah) and watt-hours (Wh). Volts designate the rated voltage, which is normally 24 V, 36 V, or 48 V. Ampere hours show the charging capacity, which usually ranges between 8 ampere-hours and 20 ampere-hours. The product of voltage and ampere hours yields the watt-hours, which ultimately indicate how much energy the battery can store. The capacities usually found on the market today range between 200 and 800 Wh, and a 300-Wh battery is a good benchmark.

Der Motor wird angetrieben von einem Akku, der vom Fahrrad abgenommen und mit einem Ladegerät an jeder Steckdose aufgeladen werden kann. Je nach Design und Marke variiert die Art der Anbringung: Manche Batterien hängen unter dem Gepäckträger, andere Hersteller verstecken sie im Rahmen, bei einigen Modellen sind sie wiederum als Trinkflasche oder Satteltasche getarnt.

Moderne Batterien nutzen elektrochemische Elemente auf der Basis von Lithium als Anodenmaterial und wiegen meist zwischen ein und drei Kilogramm. Im Schnitt muss der Akku alle 50 Kilometer neu geladen werden, die Reichweite schwankt je nach Streckenbeschaffenheit, Gewicht des Fahrers und Unterstützungsmodus.

Einige Modelle mit getriebelosen Nabenmotoren verfügen über eine elektrische Bremse, die die Bremsenergie wieder in elektrische Energie umwandelt und damit die Batterie wieder etwas auflädt. Das sogenannte Rekuperieren bringt mit heutiger Technik eine Reichweitenverlängerung von in der Regel 8 bis 15 Prozent. Eine Zukunftsvision ist das Prinzip der Energierückgewinnung während des Fahrens, also das Auskoppeln von Muskelkraft in Momenten, in denen der Fahrer einen guten Wirkungsgrad hat, und das Zurückgeben der gespeicherten Energie, wenn der Mensch einen schlechten Wirkungsgrad hat. Die Technik steckt noch in den Kinderschuhen, der erste funktionsfähige Prototyp „Bike+" (siehe Kapitel „Products", S. 202) existiert jedoch bereits.

Für den Akku gibt es Kennzahlen, anhand derer man erkennen kann, wie viel Energieinhalt und Leistungsfähigkeit die Batterie hat. In der Regel geben die Hersteller dabei Volt (V), Amperestunden (Ah) und Wattstunden (Wh) an. Volt bezeichnet die Nennspannung, die üblicherweise bei 24 V, 36 V oder 48 V liegt. Amperestunden zeigen die Ladekapazität an, die meist zwischen 8 Ah und 20 Ah liegt. Das Produkt von Volt und Amperestunde ergibt die Wattstunden, die schließlich aussagen, wie viel Energie die Batterie speichern kann. Die marktüblichen Kapazitäten liegen aktuell zwischen 200 und 800 Wh, eine 300-Wh-Batterie ist eine gute Richtgröße.

TIPS ON CARING FOR YOUR BATTERY

The battery is an e-bike's most expensive part and requires special care to ensure safe operation and a long life:*

→ If possible, recharge the battery after each use (regardless of the amount of power consumed).

→ Do not charge the battery at temperatures below 10° C.

→ Store in a cool, dry place not in danger of freezing.

→ Always fully charge the battery before storing it for extended periods and regularly recharge it during storage.

→ Always charge the battery with the charger provided for that pack. Caution: Even if the plug intended for another charger fits, the charger itself may not be compatible with your battery.

→ Never take lithium batteries onto an airplane. When transporting your bike on a car roof or rear carrier rack, always remove the batteries and carry them inside the car.

* This advice applies to all lithium, metal hydride, and lead batteries for bikes on the market in 2013.

PFLEGETIPPS

Der Akku ist das teuerste Bauteil eines E-Bikes und bedarf für den sicheren Betrieb und ein langes Leben besonderer Pflege*:

→ Die Batterie möglichst nach jeder Fahrt wieder aufladen (unabhängig von der verbrauchten Energiemenge).

→ Nicht unter 10° C aufladen.

→ Kühl und trocken lagern, aber Frost vermeiden.

→ Die Batterie vor einer längeren Lagerung immer voll laden und während der Lagerzeit regelmäßig nachladen.

→ Batterie nur mit den dafür vorgesehenen Ladegeräten laden. Achtung: Wenn der Stecker eines anderen Ladegeräts passt, muss das Ladegerät noch lange nicht zum Akku passen.

→ Lithiumbatterien nie im Flugzeug mitnehmen, beim Transport auf dem Dach- oder Heckgepäckträger eines Pkw die Batterien immer herausnehmen und im Pkw-Innenraum transportieren.

* Diese Hinweise gelten für alle 2013 im Fahrradbereich verkauften Lithium-, Nickel-Metallhydrid- und Bleibatterien.

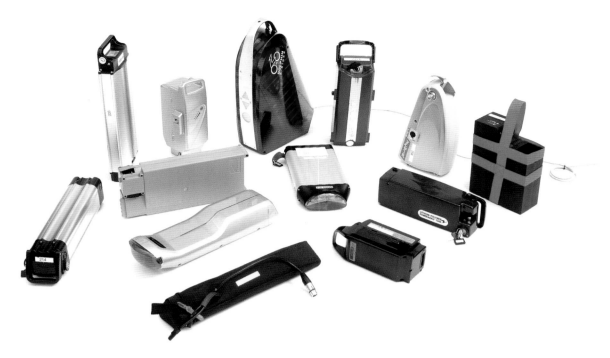

Lithium batteries have a very high energy density, which in the past often caused the batteries to catch fire. Lithium batteries for e-bikes are therefore classified as Class 9 hazardous goods and are subject to certain transport restrictions.

Batteries with state-of-the-art designs are always safe for normal use and also for what is termed "foreseeable misuse." Unfortunately, many batteries are still available that can catch fire even with ordinary misuse. Moreover, the buyer cannot rely solely on brand names, appearance or price to be sure of the battery's safety. It is therefore important to establish the battery's safety with independently monitored marks of conformity and regular follow-up inspections.

Commercial e-bike batteries that are not designed with state-of-the-art technology catch fire for three main reasons:

→ Overcharging
This happens when the battery reaches full charging capacity, but the charger continues "pumping" more energy into the battery pack.

→ Short circuit
The battery discharges all its stored energy so rapidly that the battery overheats or explodes, causing a fire. Fires can also be caused by overheated cables, which ignite the insulation and other surrounding plastic parts.

→ Physical damage
Mechanical damage to the battery, for example in a crash or by dropping the battery, can cause an internal short circuit.

The e-bike market is enormous, and the quality of the bicycles can vary widely. Certificates such as the BATSO seal help buyers make the right decision. The BATSO seal applies to battery safety and is awarded by the international Battery Safety Organization (BATSO), a joint effort between Underwriters Laboratories in the United States, TÜV Rheinland and ExtraEnergy e. V. in Germany, and the ITRI Institute in Taiwan. The batteries are tested for transport safety as well as performance during charging and use. The assessment is also based on a factory inspection as well as short circuit, drop, and crash tests. The BATSO test mark is therefore the only one that addresses safety during transport as well as during use.

Lithiumbatterien haben eine sehr hohe Energiedichte, was in der Vergangenheit öfter zu Batteriebränden geführt hat. Daher sind Lithiumbatterien von E-Bikes als Gefahrgut Klasse 9 eingestuft und dürfen nur unter gewissen Auflagen transportiert werden.

Bei Batterien, die nach dem Stand der Technik konstruiert sind, ist die Sicherheit im normalen Gebrauch und beim sogenannten vorhersehbaren Fehlgebrauch immer gewährleistet. Leider gibt es noch immer viele Batterien auf dem Markt, die sich schon bei einfachem Fehlgebrauch entzünden können. Für den Käufer ist die Sicherheit der Batterie allerdings nicht durch Markennamen, Aussehen oder den Preis der Batterie gewährleistet. Daher ist es wichtig, Sicherheit durch neutral überwachte Prüfzeichen mit regelmäßiger Nachkontrolle herzustellen.

Die drei Hauptursachen für Batteriebrände bei E-Bike-Akkus auf dem Markt, die nicht dem Stand der Technik entsprechen, sind:

→ Überladung
Diese tritt ein, wenn die maximale Ladekapazität des Akkus erreicht ist, aber das Ladegerät immer mehr Energie in die Batterie „hineinpumpt".

→ Kurzschluss
Die gesamte gespeicherte Energie des Akkus entlädt sich so schnell, dass dieser überhitzen oder explosionsartig abbrennen kann. Zum Brand kann es auch durch glühende Kabelverbindungen kommen, die die Kabelisolierung und andere umgebende Kunststoffe entzünden.

→ Physischer Schaden
Die mechanische Beschädigung der Batterie, beispielsweise ein Unfall oder das Fallenlassen des Akkus, kann zu einem inneren Kurzschluss führen.

Der Markt für E-Bikes ist riesig und die Qualität der Fahrräder sehr unterschiedlich. Zertifikate wie das BATSO-Siegel helfen bei der Orientierung. Das BATSO-Siegel bezieht sich auf die Batteriesicherheit und wird von der internationalen Battery Safety Organization (BATSO) vergeben, entstanden aus einer Zusammenarbeit der US-amerikanischen Underwriter Laboratories, des TÜV Rheinland, des ExtraEnergy e. V. und des taiwanesischen ITRI-Instituts. Die Akkus werden dabei auf ihre Transportsicherheit sowie ihr Verhalten beim Aufladen und während der Benutzung getestet. Auch eine Herstellungsinspektion zählt zur Grundlage der Beurteilung. Hinzu kommen Kurzschluss-, Fall- und Crashtests. Das BATSO-Prüfzeichen ist also das einzige, das Sicherheit sowohl beim Transport als auch beim Gebrauch zusammenfasst.

CHARGING INFRASTRUCTURE

FILL 'ER UP

Electric mobility works only if charging current can be widely found. Fortunately, this is the case in most parts of the developed world. But how do you get the electricity into the bike's battery? By using chargers—and this is where things can get problematic. We all know this dilemma from our cell phones and digital cameras: every manufacturer supplies a different charger. In 2011, Panasonic counted 73 different chargers with 99 different brands—and this number has continued to grow since then. It is therefore impossible to build a widespread network of charging stations that provide the right plug for every model. The planners of some community e-bike infrastructure projects have begun using 230-volt grounding outlets. However, this means that e-bike riders have to take their own chargers along on a ride and store both the battery and charger in a water-proof place.

The standard plug developed by the EnergyBus Consortium for charging light electric vehicles has been available since 2012. Like the USB port on computers, this plug is compatible with all chargers that comply with the standard. Standardization also benefits the environment, since the charger can be used universally for multiple vehicles, and consumers do not have to purchase a new charger whenever they buy a new vehicle. This development also motivates the European Union to expedite their standardization process.

Another argument in favor of standardized charging infrastructure is the long time it takes to charge most OEM chargers—from two to four hours. This charging time is impractical for touring. Who wants to sit next to their bike for two hours and wait for it to charge? With standardized charging infrastructure and modern battery technology, a battery can be recharged in five minutes for a 6-mile range. A 15-minute rest stop is all it would take to recharge the battery for another 19 miles. For cycle tourism, this would provide a more or less unlimited range, since the average biker usually needs to take a breather every 19 miles in any case.

A battery replacement system currently provides the fastest energy boost. This approach is available only in tourism regions that require rental agencies to use a particular e-bike model. Tourists who wish to go on a bike tour, rent an e-bike and exchange the empty battery for a fully charged one at excursion destinations and hotels, much the way mail carriages of an earlier age would replace tired horses with well-rested ones at postal stations. Currently, this system works only as an isolated approach in certain regions.

CHARGE & LOCK CABLE

LOCK   LOAD

Another idea is to use the EnergyBus Charge-Lock Cable, which combines a secure lock with charging capability. Bikers take along their own bicycle lock, which at first glance looks like an ordinary cable lock. Inside, however, is a hidden EnergyBus cable, which not only protects the bike against theft when connected to a compatible bike stand, but also charges the bike at the same time. If a thief tries to cut through the cable, the electronics detect the attempted theft and either disable the bike's electric components or notify the owner of the theft. The charging cable provides greater security than a purely mechanical lock.

Despite these unresolved charging infrastructure issues, the electric two-wheeler has already gained enormous popularity throughout the world, with more than 150 million vehicles on the road. User-friendly infrastructure could provide another significant boost to the popularity of these bikes.

Elektronische Mobilität ist nur möglich, wenn an jeder Ecke Strom fließt. Das ist in den meisten Regionen der westlichen Welt glücklicherweise der Fall. Aber wie kommt der Strom in die Akkus der Bikes? Über Ladegeräte, und die sind das Problem. Das Dilemma ist bestens von Handys und Digitalkameras bekannt: Jeder Hersteller liefert sein eigenes Ladegerät. Eine Zählung von Panasonic ergab 2011 allein 73 verschiedene Ladestecker von 99 Marken. Die Zahl nimmt aktuell immer noch zu. Das macht den Aufbau eines flächendeckenden Netzes an Ladestationen, die für jedes Modell den passenden Stecker anbieten, unmöglich. Bei einigen kommunalen E-Bike-Infrastrukturprojekten greifen die Planer auf 230-Volt-Schuko-Steckdosen zurück. Für E-Bike-Fahrer bedeutet das allerdings, dass auf der Tour das eigene Ladegerät mitgenommen und der Akku zusammen mit dem Ladegerät an einem regensicheren Ort aufbewahrt werden muss.

Seit 2012 gibt es den vom EnergyBus-Konsortium entwickelten Standardstecker für das Laden von Leichtelektrofahrzeugen. Wie beim USB-Anschluss am Computer ist dieser Stecker kompatibel mit allen Ladegeräten, die dem Standard folgen. Standardisierung bringt auch für die Umwelt Vorteile, weil das Ladegerät universell für mehrere Fahrzeuge genutzt werden kann und so bei einem neuen Fahrzeug nicht immer ein neues Ladegerät mit angeschafft werden muss. Dies ist auch ein Antrieb für die Europäische Union, die Standardisierung zu forcieren.

Ein weiteres Argument für eine standardisierte Ladeinfrastruktur sind die mit zwei bis vier Stunden recht langen Ladezeiten der meisten Originalladegeräte. Das ist unpraktisch für Touren, denn wer möchte schon zwei Stunden neben seinem Bike ausharren, bis es wieder aufgeladen ist? Mit einer standardisierten Ladeinfrastruktur und der heutigen Batterietechnik ist es möglich, in fünf Minuten zehn Kilometer Reichweite nachzuladen. Bei einer kleinen Rast von 15 Minuten wären also 30 Kilometer nachgeladen. Damit wäre die Reichweite in der touristischen Anwendung quasi unendlich, da sich der Durchschnittsradler in der Regel nach 30 Kilometern Fahrt ohnehin eine kleine Verschnaufpause gönnt.

Aktuell ist der schnellste Energieschub ein System, das auf dem Akku-Tausch basiert. Dieses Prinzip wird nur in Urlaubsregionen realisiert, die sich auf den Verleih eines bestimmten E-Bike-Modells festgelegt haben. Hier leiht sich der radelwillige Tourist ein E-Bike und wechselt an Ausflugszielen und Hotels die leere Batterie gegen eine aufgeladene aus, ähnlich wie zur Zeit der Postkutschen an den Poststationen die müden Pferde gegen ausgeruhte getauscht werden konnten. Dieses System funktioniert momentan nur als regionale Insellösung.

Eine andere Idee ist das EnergyBus-Ladeschloss-Kabel: Es vereint sicheres Abschließen und Aufladen. Die Fahrer nehmen dabei ihr eigenes Fahrradschloss mit, welches auf den ersten Blick wie ein gewöhnliches Kabelschloss aussieht. Allerdings ist darin ein EnergyBus-Kabel verborgen. Dieses sichert das E-Bike beim Anschließen an einen dafür vorgesehenen Fahrradständer nicht nur gegen Diebstahl, sondern lädt es gleichzeitig auf. Sollten Diebe auf die Idee kommen, das Kabel zu zerschneiden, erkennt die Elektronik das. Die elektrischen Komponenten des Bikes könnten sich dann selbst blockieren oder auch den Eigentümer über den Diebstahl informieren. Das Ladekabel ermöglicht eine höhere Sicherheit als ein rein mechanisches Schloss.

Das elektrische Zweirad hat es trotz der noch unzureichend geklärten Ladeinfrastruktur weltweit schon zu einer erheblichen Verbreitung mit mehr als 150 Millionen Fahrzeugen auf der Straße geschafft. Eine nutzerfreundliche Infrastruktur könnte der Verbreitung noch einen deutlichen Schub geben.

10

REASONS
WHY eBIKES
ARE COOL

BETTER MOBILITY

1

When there's yet another traffic jam during rush hour and cars are creeping along inch by inch, it's clearly an advantage to be an e-bike rider. You can bypass the congestion by weaving in and out of traffic or passing cars on the right or left or—better yet—by simply speeding past on a bike path.

Wenn zur Rushhour mal wieder nichts geht und die bunten Metallkarossen wie eine zähe Masse Zentimeter für Zentimeter weiterfließen, ist man als E-Bike-Fahrer klar im Vorteil. Man schlängelt sich schlicht dazwischen oder daneben durch den Verkehr oder fährt auf dem Radweg einfach vorbei.

FREE PARKING

You'll never have to hunt for a parking spot again, because you'll always find a place to park your e-bike, whether in your office or locked to a lamp post. And the fear that your little beauty might fall victim to theft is overblown: Many e-bikes come equipped with very sophisticated and reliable anti-theft systems.

Die Parkplatzsuche hat ein Ende, denn für ein E-Bike findet sich immer ein Stellplatz, ob am Laternenpfahl oder im Büro. Und die Angst, dass das Prachtstück Langfingern zum Opfer fällt, ist unbegründet: Viele E-Bikes verfügen über eine sehr ausgereifte und zuverlässige Diebstahlsicherung.

2

SAVE MONEY

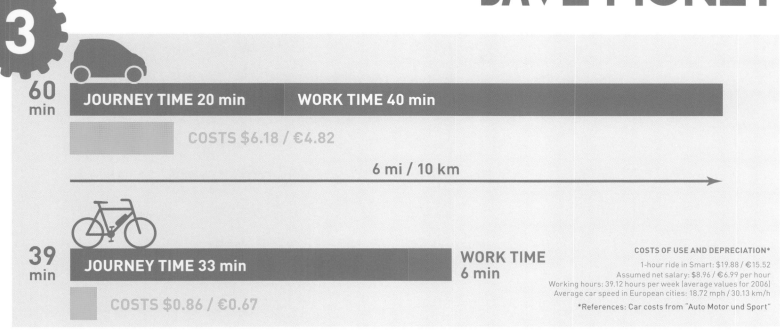

3

60 min

JOURNEY TIME 20 min | WORK TIME 40 min

COSTS $6.18 / €4.82

6 mi / 10 km

39 min

JOURNEY TIME 33 min | WORK TIME 6 min

COSTS $0.86 / €0.67

COSTS OF USE AND DEPRECIATION*
1-hour ride in Smart: $19.88 / €15.52
Assumed net salary: $8.96 / €6.99 per hour
Working hours: 39.12 hours per week (average values for 2006)
Average car speed in European cities: 18.72 mph / 30.13 km/h

*References: Car costs from "Auto Motor und Sport"

E-bikes are not only much cheaper to buy than cars, they are unbeatable when it comes to maintenance. The annual cost of charging an e-bike's battery is about the same as eating out at a restaurant.

Ein E-Bike ist nicht nur in der Anschaffung günstiger als ein Auto, sondern auch im Unterhalt unschlagbar. Die Aufladung kostet pro Jahr nicht mehr als ein Restaurantbesuch.

FRESH AIR

4

Exhaust fumes cause blankets of smog to settle over our cities. E-bikes do not generate fine particulates and cause fewer CO_2 emissions than cars. That not only saves money when it comes to the fees for emissions stickers or congestion charges, but also helps improve the air quality in our big cities.

Autoabgase sorgen für große Dunstglocken über unseren Städten. E-Bikes erzeugen keinen Feinstaub und verursachen weniger CO_2-Emissionen als Autos. Das spart nicht nur die Gebühren für Umweltplaketten oder City-Maut, sondern sorgt auch für frische Luft in den Metropolen.

BE INDEPENDENT

The subway is on strike again, and just before summer vacation gasoline prices have shot sky high. Yet e-bike owners couldn't care less. They don't need anything or anyone except for a power outlet and maybe some nice weather. Even out in the country, people without a driver's license don't have to be hermits anymore. Five miles to the next town or twenty miles to the county seat are a snap with an e-bike!

Die U-Bahn streikt mal wieder und kurz vor Ostern teilen sich die Spritpreise eine Atmosphärenschicht mit Felix Baumgartner. Das ist den E-Bike-Fahrern egal. Sie brauchen nichts und niemanden außer einer Steckdose und vielleicht gutem Wetter. Auch auf dem Land müssen führerscheinlose Menschen keine Eremiten mehr sein. 10 Kilometer ins Nachbardorf oder 30 Kilometer in die Kreisstadt sind per E-Bike ein Klacks!

5

COUCH-POTATO? NOT ANY LONGER!

E-bikes have a knack of winning over even the most devout couch potatoes. Once you start pedaling an e-bike, you'll become intoxicated by the speed. And you'll relish the joy of being on the go without sweat beading up on your forehead. Biking at least 30 minutes a day extends your life by eight healthy years.

E-Bikes haben die Eigenschaft, selbst die größten Stubenhocker in Bewegung zu bringen. Einmal getreten, packt einen schnell der Rausch der Geschwindigkeit. Und die Freude, ohne Schweißperlen auf der Stirn fix unterwegs zu sein. Zumal 30 Minuten Radfahren am Tag das Leben um acht gesunde Jahre verlängern.

6

BE A CLIMATE HERO

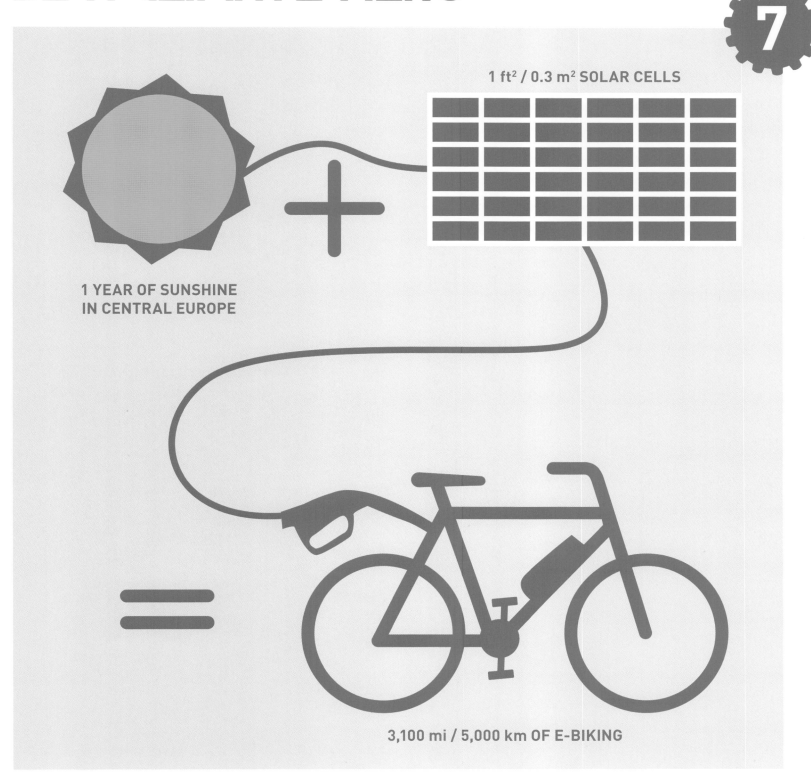

1 ft² / 0.3 m² SOLAR CELLS

1 YEAR OF SUNSHINE
IN CENTRAL EUROPE

3,100 mi / 5,000 km OF E-BIKING

The more car trips are replaced by e-bikes, the easier it will be to achieve mandatory reductions in CO_2 emissions. A solar panel just one square foot in size is enough to power an e-bike for 3,100 miles every year. No other vehicle is as energy efficient. E-bike riders really are environmental heroes.

Je mehr Autofahrten durch E-Bikes ersetzt werden, umso leichter können die vorgeschriebenen CO_2-Einsparungen erreicht werden. Umgerechnet genügt eine Solaranlage von 0,3 Quadratmeter Größe, um jedes Jahr 5000 Kilometer E-Bike zu fahren. Kein anderes Fahrzeug ist so energieeffizient. E-Bike-Fahrer sind also unsere Umwelthelden.

ELECTRIC DESIGN

Grandma's bike is so yesterday. Today's bikes have power, can handle all sorts of terrain, and have developed their own design language. There is something to appeal to every taste. You're always well dressed with the right e-bike.

Oma-Vehikel war gestern. Die Bikes von heute haben Power, rasen über Stock und Stein und haben ihre ganz eigene Designsprache entwickelt. Für jeden Geschmack dürfte etwas dabei sein. Mit dem richtigen E-Bike ist man einfach immer gut angezogen.

ACCESSIBILITY

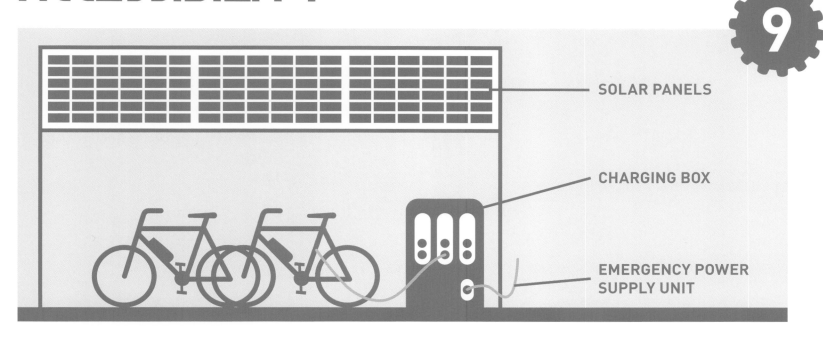

SOLAR PANELS

CHARGING BOX

EMERGENCY POWER
SUPPLY UNIT

City administrators are beginning to react to city traffic issues, a problem on a massive scale. In addition to new parking regulations, networks of bicycle rental locations and secure parking options with charging stations are expanding. Of course, riders can also easily charge their bikes at work or at home. You'll never again have to say: "I have to go gas the car." The gas station is now at home—which couldn't be any more convenient.

Die Stadtverwaltungen reagieren langsam auf die immer massiver werdenden Probleme des Stadtverkehrs. Neben neuen Parkregelungen wird auch das Netz von Fahrradverleihen und sicheren Parkmöglichkeiten mit Aufladestationen ausgebaut. Ansonsten einfach im Büro oder zu Hause aufladen. Nie wieder der Satz: „Ich muss nur noch schnell zur Tankstelle." Die Tankstelle ist jetzt zu Hause und da kommt man spätestens am Ende des Tages immer vorbei!

EASE AND SIMPLICITY

Buy and ride, that's how simple things are with an e-bike. There's no learning curve with the popular 15-mile-per-hour models. Large or small, young or old, with or without physical impairments—anyone can ride an e-bike.

Kaufen und Fahren ist die Devise bei E-Bikes. Die gängigen 25-Stundenkilometer-Modelle können von jedem gefahren werden, ohne dass die Benutzung neu erlernt werden müsste. Ob klein oder groß, jung oder alt, eingeschränkt oder nicht – das E-Bike beherrscht einfach jeder.

10

PRODUCTS & PORTRAITS

BIKE CITY

SWIX MORGAN DENNY ON
KALKHOFF // TASMAN TOUR C8

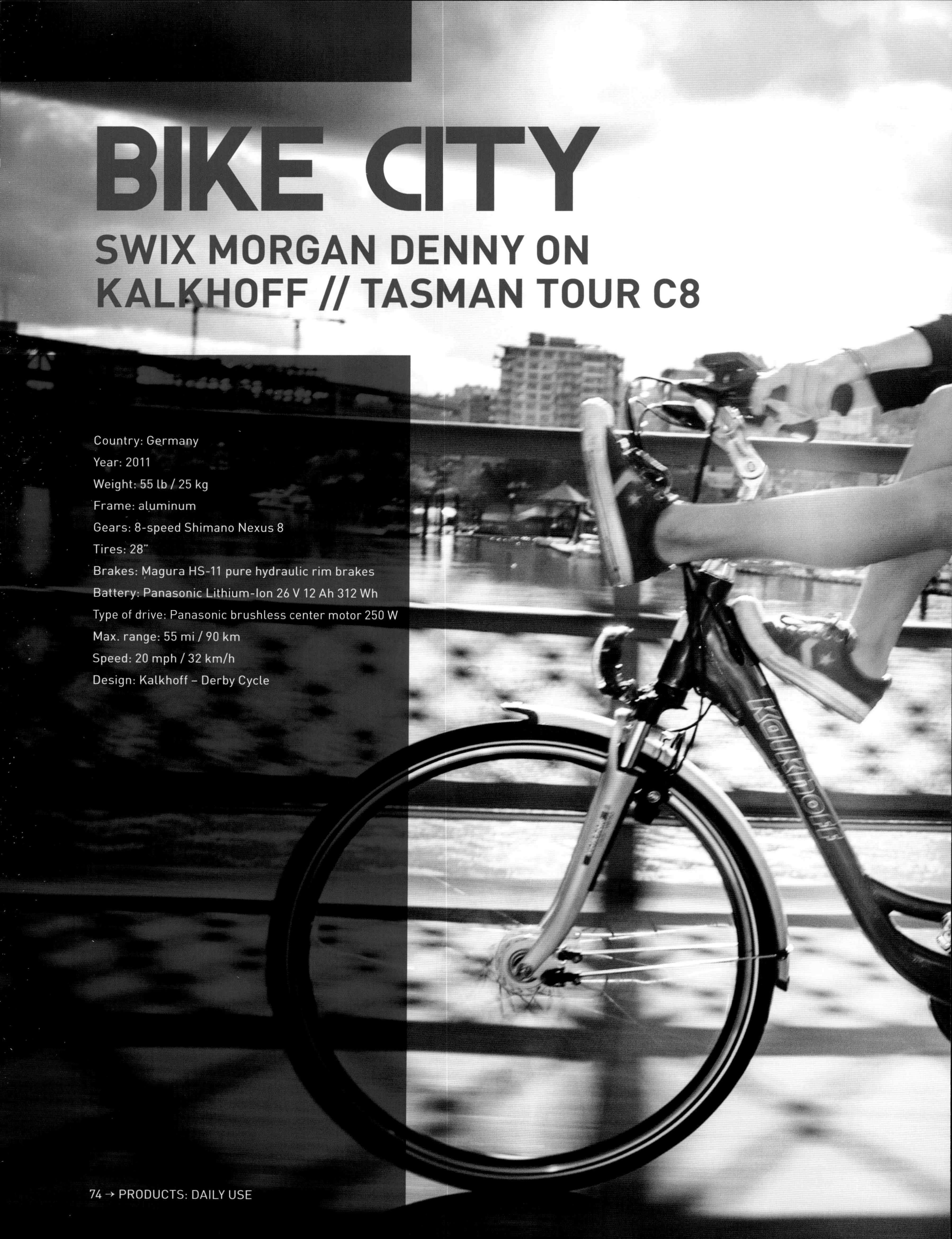

Country: Germany

Year: 2011

Weight: 55 lb / 25 kg

Frame: aluminum

Gears: 8-speed Shimano Nexus 8

Tires: 28"

Brakes: Magura HS-11 pure hydraulic rim brakes

Battery: Panasonic Lithium-Ion 26 V 12 Ah 312 Wh

Type of drive: Panasonic brushless center motor 250 W

Max. range: 55 mi / 90 km

Speed: 20 mph / 32 km/h

Design: Kalkhoff – Derby Cycle

Swix feels right at home in Portland, Oregon. The physical therapist has lived in her dream city for six years. She likes the diversity of Portland, the openness of its approximately 600,000 inhabitants, as well as the city's alternative spirit. Discussions with her friends tend to revolve around microbreweries, healthy eating, and a responsible and conscious lifestyle.

Hardly anyone knows that Portland is the second most popular bicycle city in the world after Amsterdam—even coming in ahead of Copenhagen. A network of bicycle paths extending roughly 185 miles makes bicycling easy for residents of this liberal city. The city administration estimates that 16% of Portland residents bike to work. Employers support this trend by equipping their businesses with secure bicycle storage areas, changing rooms, and showers. The weather, however, does not seem as supportive of this mode of outdoor transportation: On the northwest coast of the United States, it rains an average of 271 days a year. Yet that sounds worse than it actually is: For the most part, the rain amounts to a brief drizzle—certainly no hindrance for Portland's avid cyclists, and that naturally includes Swix.

YOU'LL ALMOST NEVER SEE SWIX HOLDING CAR KEYS.

Swix' real name is Morgan Denny. A friend gave her the nickname because she always wears the classic earmuffs made by Swiss ski company Swix. You'll almost never see Swix holding car keys, so it comes as no surprise that she has more than just one bicycle at home. Her latest acquisition is a German e-bike, which she now rides daily to her practice in downtown Portland. In the mornings when she is still sleepy and speed is of the essence, she uses the Power on Demand mode, which provides electric motor assistance on her way to work. On her way home in the evenings she doesn't switch on the battery at all, choosing to ride in Pedal Assist mode. That means straight biking using just her muscle strength to ensure that she reaps the health benefits for her body. She only drives her car if she cannot avoid it—including once a year to visit the Burning Man music and art festival held in the Nevada desert.

Denny likes to browse through Portland's flea markets to purchase odds and ends made of various materials, which she then uses to make "mutant toys": artwork from wood, plastic, and even rubber. She gifts her new creations made of scrap materials to friends and coworkers. If you ask this dynamic Portland transplant what she is most passionate about apart from recycling art and her e-bike, she doesn't need to think long about her answer: the EcoJaunt project. An avid environmentalist, Denny just returned from a one-year tour through the United States. She took to the road in a van converted specifically for the trip. Equipped with a variety of cameras and searching for America's soul, Swix and her friend Travis used videos and a blog to report about unconventional approaches to generating energy, organic farming, new building materials, organic animal husbandry, and alternative medicine.

Swix sees herself as a pioneer. She hopes that her travelogues will entertain and inspire others to adopt a more conscious lifestyle. Her greatest desire? To win over the hearts of others so they too will embrace her ideal of sustainability.

Swix fühlt sich in Portland, Oregon, sehr gut aufgehoben. Seit sechs Jahren lebt die Physiotherapeutin hier und hat ihre Traumstadt gefunden. Sie mag die Bandbreite von Portland, die Offenheit der rund 600.000 Einwohner, den alternativen Spirit der Stadt. Die Diskussionen bei ihren Freunden kreisen um Kleinbrauereien, gesundes Essen und die Frage nach einem verantwortlichen und bewussten Lebensstil.

Kaum einer weiß, dass Portland nach Amsterdam die zweitbeliebteste Fahrradstadt der Welt ist, noch vor Kopenhagen. Ein knapp 300 Kilometer langes Netz aus Fahrradwegen macht den Einwohnern der liberalen Stadt das Radeln leicht. Die Verwaltung schätzt, dass 16 Prozent der Portländer mit dem Rad zur Arbeit kommen. Das unterstützen die Arbeitgeber, indem sie ihre Unternehmen mit Fahrradkäfigen, Umkleiden und Duschen ausstatten. Was scheinbar gegen die Fortbewegung unter freiem Himmel spricht, ist dagegen das Wetter: An durchschnittlich 271 Tagen im Jahr regnet es hier an der Nordwestküste der USA. Das hört sich allerdings ungemütlicher an, als es ist: Meistens handelt es sich nur um kurzen Nieselregen, kein Hindernis für die leidenschaftlichen Fahrradfahrer dieser Stadt, zu denen Swix gehört.

Swix heißt eigentlich Morgan Denny. Den Spitznamen hat ihr eine Freundin verpasst, weil sie zum Fahrradfahren immer die klassischen Ohrwärmer der Schweizer Skifirma trägt. Natürlich hat Swix, die man so gut wie nie mit einem Autoschlüssel in der Hand sieht, mehr als nur ein Fahrrad zu Hause. Ihre neueste Errungenschaft ist ein deutsches E-Bike, mit dem sie inzwischen täglich zu ihrer Praxis in Downtown Portland fährt. Morgens, wenn sie noch verschlafen ist und sich beeilen muss, nutzt sie den „Power on Demand"-Modus, mit Zusatzhilfe der Batterie. Anders am Abend, auf dem Heimweg: Da schaltet sie die Batterie erst gar nicht an und fährt im „Pedal Assist"-Modus. Das bedeutet dann pures Fahrradfahren mit Muskelkraft, damit sie auch etwas für ihren Körper tut. Ihr Auto fährt sie nur, wenn es wirklich nicht anders geht – und natürlich einmal im Jahr zum Musik- und Kunstfestival „Burning Man" in der Wüste von Nevada.

Morgan klappert gerne die Trödelmärkte der Stadt ab, um Krimskrams aus unterschiedlichen Materialien zu erstehen. Daraus bastelt sich dann „Mutant Toys": Spielsachen oder Kunst aus Holz, Plastik oder auch Gummi. Die neuen Kreationen aus Altmaterial verschenkt sie an Freunde und Arbeitskollegen. Fragt man die dynamische Frau, wofür ihr Herz neben Recycling-Kunst und ihrem E-Bike am lautesten schlägt, muss sie nicht lange überlegen: das Projekt EcoJaunt. Die Umweltschützerin ist eben erst von einer einjährigen Rundreise durch die USA zurückgekehrt. Unterwegs war sie mit einem eigens dafür umgebauten Kleinbus. Mit diversen Kameras ausgerüstet und auf der Suche nach der amerikanischen Seele, berichtete Swix in Videos und ihrem Blog über unkonventionelle Möglichkeiten der Energiegewinnung, ökologische Landwirtschaft, neue Bausubstanzen, biologische Tierhaltung und alternative Medizin.

Swix sieht sich als Wegbereiterin. Sie hofft, dass ihre Reiseberichte auf unterhaltsame Weise zu einem bewussten Lebensstil inspirieren. Ihr größter Wunsch? Die Herzen ihrer Landsleute für ihr Ideal von Nachhaltigkeit zu gewinnen.

STYLISH SHOPPING

GAZELLE // MISS GRACE INNERGY

Miss Grace Innergy is an e-bike designed especially for women who want to be able to transport heavier loads. Riders can easily attach their cargo to the bike's front carrier and rear rack located over the front and rear wheels. Extra-wide tires offer a high degree of stability even when transporting the bulkiest objects. At 61.5 pounds, this bike is no featherweight even without any freight, but the two-wheel drive technology supports both wheels, offering a fast and easy ride. As a market leader in the Netherlands, in 1992 this Dutch bicycle manufacturer was awarded the "Royal" title in honor of its 100th birthday.

Miss Grace Innergy ist ein E-Bike speziell für Damen, die viel transportieren möchten. Über dem Vorder- und Hinterrad können diese ihre Lasten problemlos befestigen. Breite Reifen sorgen auch bei hoher Ladung für Stabilität. Mit 28 Kilogramm ist das Rad auch ohne Gepäck kein Fliegengewicht, aber die Two-wheel-drive-Technologie unterstützt beide Räder, sodass man mühelos und schnell unterwegs ist. Der niederländische Fahrradhersteller darf sich übrigens seit 1992 aufgrund seines über 100-jährigen Bestehens und seiner Marktführerposition mit dem Titel „königlich" schmücken.

Country: Netherlands // Year: 2012 // Weight: 61.5 lb / 28 kg // Frame: aluminum // Gears: 7-speed Shimano Nexus freewheel hub
Tires: 28" // Brakes: front: Shimano V-brakes, rear: Shimano Nexus roller brakes // Battery: BMZ / Sanyo Lithium-Ion 36 V 7 Ah 256 Wh
Type of drive: Kreuzer front wheel hub motor 250 W // Max. range: 50 mi / 80 km // Speed: 15 mph / 25 km/h // Design: Koninklijke Gazelle N.V.

THE BIKE NEXT DOOR

CANNONDALE // CANNONDALE E-SERIES

This bike from the Cannondale E-Series, winner of the 2012 E-Bike contest in the Netherlands, has a classic appeal and offers great riding stability. The Cannondale-specific HeadShok fork on the front wheel offers agility and safety while handling curves. With four different modes (Eco, Tour, Sport, and Speed) for varying degrees of assistance, riders will be able to find the right challenge for every occasion. Located on the East Coast of the U.S., Cannondale manufactures high-quality bicycles, motocross bikes, and ATVs and is the official supplier to many professional cyclists and triathletes.

Das Bike aus der Cannondale E-Series, Gewinner des E-Bike Contest 2012 in den Niederlanden, ist durch eine klassische Optik und eine hohe Fahrstabilität gekennzeichnet. Die Cannondale-spezifische HeadShok-Gabel am Vorderrad sorgt für Wendigkeit und Sicherheit in den Kurven. Unter den vier Unterstützungsmodi Eco, Tour, Sport und Speed sollte jeder Fahrer zu jedem Anlass die richtige Herausforderung finden. Der Hersteller hochwertiger Fahrräder, Motocrossmaschinen und Quads an der US-amerikanischen Ostküste ist Ausrüster zahlreicher Radsportler und Triathleten.

Country: USA // Year: 2011 // Weight: 49.5 lb / 22.5 kg // Frame: 6061 aluminum
Gears: 8-speed Shimano Alfine / 9-speed Shimano SLX // Tires: 28" // Brakes: Magura MT2 hydraulic disc brakes
Battery: Bosch 36 V 8 Ah 288 Wh // Type of drive: Bosch center motor 250 W // Max. range: 85 mi / 140 km
Speed: 15 mph / 25 km/h // Design: Cannondale

REAL EUROPEAN

ROCK MACHINE // POWERFLEX D24T

This elegant women's bike is dominated by compelling yet restrained aesthetics. The battery remains discreetly concealed under the rear rack, where it inconspicuously waits to be used. When needed, it supports the rider's pedaling with 15 levels of electric assistance. What may not be apparent in this pearl-gray gem is that it is truly multicultural. It was designed in the Netherlands; it is manufactured in the Czech Republic; and it is marketed from Switzerland.

Dieses elegante Damenrad wird von einer bestechend unaufdringlichen Ästhetik dominiert. Der Akku bleibt dezent wie ein Gentleman unter dem Gepäckträger verborgen und wartet dort unauffällig auf seinen Einsatz. Dann schaltet er sich in 15 fein abgestimmten Stufen zur Muskelkraft der Fahrerin hinzu. Was man dem perlgrauen Schmuckstück nicht ansieht: Es ist ein richtiges Multikulti-Bike. Das Design stammt aus den Niederlanden, produziert wird es in Tschechien und vertrieben über die Schweiz.

Country: Developed in NL / Produced in CZ // Year: 2011 // Weight: 50.5 lb / 23 kg
Frame: aluminum 6061-T6 // Gears: 24-speed Shimano Acera // Tires: 29" // Brakes: Tektro Alloy V-brakes
Battery: Panasonic Lithium-Ion 25.2 V 17.4 Ah 438 Wh // Type of drive: Dapu Motors Japan rear wheel hub motor 250 W
Max. range: 110 mi / 180 km // Speed: 15 mph / 25 km/h // Design: BFI Bike Fun International

小沼あみ

AMI KONUMA ON
SANYO // CY – SPA600NA

Country: Japan

Weight: 50.3 lb / 23 kg

Frame: aluminum

Gears: 3

Tires: 26"

Brakes: front: side-pull caliper type, rear: roller brake

Battery: Lithium-Ion 25.2 V 5.7 Ah 144 Wh

Type of drive: brushless front wheel hub motor 250 W

Max. range: 45 mi / 70 km

Speed: 15 mph / 25 km/h

The Hachiōji campus is located on the edge of Tokyo. The extensive grounds are home to several of Tokyo's universities, and primarily younger students are taught here. One such student is Ami Konuma; she originally comes from the prefecture of Gunma in the heart of Japan's main island. The twenty-one-year-old studies art at Tama Art University, majoring in photography. She is currently involved in information design, programming, and kinetic art. She is working on a light installation and she takes photographs nearly every day.

The campus in Hachiōji is located on a hill, and the commute to Ami's university is nothing but up and down. It takes a long time to walk there, and biking is strenuous. At some point, Ami got tired of the grind and bought herself an e-bike. "The first time I rode up the hill to the university, I felt like a child being pushed from behind," she recalls. Since then, she rides her bike to class every day and she only needs 15 minutes to get there. "Riding a normal bike up the streets to school was really hard work. It's much easier and more comfortable with the e-bike." When she needs to bring books and work materials from home to her classes, she is especially happy that she no longer has to rely on her muscle strength alone to transport it all.

Her roommate and best friend Mao Kobori has the same e-bike. The two used to attend the same high school, and now they live and study together. Ami was so enthusiastic about the sleek design and the boost when climbing hills, she recommended the same model to her friend. Mao decided on a different color. When they have classes that start at the same time, the two friends now zip up the long hill side by side.

"Not many people my age own an e-bike. My friends think it's something special and wish they had one too. Everyone here on campus gets sick of dealing with the hills every day," Ami remarks.

I CAN'T IMAGINE LIVING WITHOUT AN E-BIKE ANYMORE.

Like many people who ride e-bikes, she wishes that the battery were lighter. "I understand why the batteries are heavy, but my bike weighs 54 pounds!" On the other hand, Ami is happy that she no longer has to carry as much, because the e-bike relieves her of the load. "That makes me feel safer. Sometimes I don't come home from the university until late, when it's already dark. If I get the creeps, all I need to do is push a button and I'm home before I know it." Ami doesn't ride in downtown Tokyo, though, and she prefers to take public transportation when it's snowing or raining hard. She charges the battery on her e-bike every other day. "I charge it at night while I'm sleeping—that's the easiest way. All in all, the e-bike is very convenient and it has made my life so much easier. I can't imagine living without an e-bike anymore." In her free time, however, Ami doesn't ride her e-bike much. She would rather watch movies or play basketball.

Der Hachiōji-Campus liegt am Rande Tokios. Einige Universitäten der japanischen Hauptstadt haben auf dem weitläufigen Gelände ihre Fakultäten, vor allem jüngere Studenten werden hier unterrichtet. So auch Ami Konuma, die ursprünglich aus der Präfektur Gunma stammt, im Herzen der Hauptinsel. Die 21-Jährige studiert Kunst an der Tama Art University mit dem Hauptfach Fotografie. Momentan beschäftigt sie sich mit Informationsdesign, Programmieren und kinetischer Kunst. Sie arbeitet an einer Lichtinstallation und natürlich fotografiert sie fast jeden Tag.

Der Campus in Hachiōji befindet sich auf einem Hügel, der Weg zu ihrer Fakultät ist ein einziges Auf und Ab. Laufen dauert lange und mit dem Fahrrad ist der Weg kräftezehrend. Irgendwann war Ami die Plackerei leid und kaufte sich ein E-Bike. „Als ich das erste Mal damit den Berg zur Uni hochfuhr, fühlte ich mich wie ein Kind, das von hinten angeschoben wird", erinnert sie sich. Seitdem nutzt die Studentin das E-Bike täglich, um zu ihren Kursen zu kommen. Jetzt braucht sie nur noch 15 Minuten. „Mit einem normalen Rad die Straßen zur Uni hochzufahren war wirklich harte Arbeit. Mit dem E-Bike ist es viel leichter und bequemer." Vor allem, wenn sie Bücher und Arbeitsmaterialien von zu Hause mit in die Kurse nehmen will, ist sie froh, dass sie nicht mehr alles nur mit Muskelkraft bewegen muss.

Ihre Mitbewohnerin und beste Freundin Mao Kobori fährt das gleiche Rad. Früher gingen die beiden auf dieselbe Highschool, jetzt wohnen und studieren sie zusammen. Weil Ami so begeistert von dem schlichten Design und der Unterstützung bei den Steigungen war, hat sie ihrer Freundin dieses Modell empfohlen. Mao entschied sich allerdings für eine andere Farbe. Wenn ihre Kurse zur selben Zeit beginnen, düsen die beiden Freundinnen jetzt Seite an Seite den langen Hügel hoch.

„Nicht viele Leute in meinem Alter besitzen ein E-Bike. Meine Freunde und Bekannten halten es für etwas Besonderes und hätten auch gern eines. Jeder hier am Campus ist genervt von der täglichen Anstrengung", weiß Ami.

Wie viele E-Bike-Rider wünscht auch sie sich, dass der Akku leichter sein sollte. „Ich verstehe ja, warum die Akkus schwer sind, aber mein Rad wiegt 24,5 Kilogramm!" Auf der anderen Seite ist Ami froh, dass sie jetzt nicht mehr so viel schleppen muss, weil das E-Bike ihr das Gewicht abnimmt. „Und es gibt mir ein Gefühl von Sicherheit. Manchmal komme ich erst spätabends, wenn es dunkel ist, aus der Uni. Wenn ich mich dann grusele, drücke ich einfach einen Knopf und bin schnell zu Hause." In Tokio selbst fährt Ami aber nicht und auch bei starkem Regen oder Schnee nimmt sie lieber die öffentlichen Verkehrsmittel. Alle zwei Tage lädt sie den Akku ihres E-Bikes auf. „Das mache ich nachts, wenn ich schlafe. Das ist am bequemsten. Überhaupt ist das E-Bike eine sehr bequeme Sache; es hat mein Leben wirklich leichter gemacht. Ich kann mir gar nicht mehr vorstellen, ohne E-Bike zu leben." Nur zum Spaß, in ihrer Freizeit, benutzt Ami das E-Bike jedoch kaum. Da schaut sie sich lieber Filme an oder spielt Basketball.

THE KING OF DATA

VSF FAHRRADMANUFAKTUR // P-300

The roots of this Northern German company can be traced back to the former Association of Independent Cycle Dealers, an organization of independent bicycle shops. This group resulted from the desire to promote the bicycle as a means of transportation. It is difficult to determine whether progress has been made in this regard. However, there's no doubt that the speedometer on the P-300 measures personal progress: It displays the current speed, average speed, maximum speed, route, trip distance, total miles, remaining range, and engine power. A USB interface makes it possible to charge smartphones and MP3 players while riding.

Die Wurzeln des norddeutschen Unternehmens liegen im ehemaligen Verbund Selbstverwalteter Fahrradbetriebe, einem Zusammenschluss freier Fahrradläden. Er entstand aus der Motivation heraus, das Rad als Verkehrsmittel zu fördern. Ob diesbezüglich Fortschritte erzielt wurden, ist schwer messbar. Dafür misst der Tacho des P-300 die persönlichen Fortschritte: Aktuelle Geschwindigkeit, Durchschnittsgeschwindigkeit, maximale Geschwindigkeit, Fahrstrecke, Tageskilometer, Gesamtkilometer, Restreichweite und Motorleistung werden angezeigt. Über eine USB-Schnittstelle werden Smartphones und MP3-Player während der Fahrt geladen.

Country: Germany // Year: 2013 // Weight: 53.5 lb / 24.4 kg // Frame: aluminum

Gears: 8-speed Shimano Nexus with freewheel // Tires: 28" // Brakes: Magura HS11 hydraulic rim brakes

Battery: Bosch Lithium-Ion 36 V 8.2 Ah 300 Wh // Type of drive: Bosch center motor 250 W

Max. range: 90 mi / 145 km // Speed: 15 mph / 25 km/h // Design: Rainer Gerdes

A SAFER RIDE

ZEMO // ZE-8

With this bike, riding safety is a top priority: Hydraulic disc brakes ensure that riders can safely stop even while going downhill or in wet conditions; bright front and rear lights illuminate the road and provide for excellent visibility, even for the rider. The center motor, mounted low, adds stability, and means flat tires can be quickly and easily repaired. A beautifully curved single-tube frame makes it easy for riders to climb on. The battery is safely and discretely attached below the rear rack, not distracting from the clear and sophisticated appearance of the bike. This premium bicycle offers five levels of assistance; depending on the rider's preference, the economical Bosch system can add from 30% to 250% to the rider's own muscle strength.

Die Fahrsicherheit steht bei diesem Bike an erster Stelle: Hydraulische Scheibenbremsen sorgen dafür, dass man auch bergab und bei Nässe sicher zum Halten kommt, helle Front- und Rücklichter machen den Weg und den Fahrer selbst gut sichtbar. Der tief angelegte Mittelmotor stabilisiert und Reifenpannen sind schnell und einfach behoben. Ein schön geschwungener Einrohrrahmen erleichtert zudem das Aufsteigen. Unterhalb des Gepäckträgers ist der Akku angebracht, so sicher und dezent, dass die klare, edle Optik des Bikes nicht zerstört wird. Das Premiumrad bietet fünf fein abgestimmte Unterstützungsstufen und je nach Wunsch fügt das sparsame Bosch-System 30 bis 250 Prozent der eigenen Muskelkraft hinzu.

Country: Germany // Year: 2013 // Weight: 54.5 lb / 24.7 kg // Frame: 6061 aluminum hydropress forming
Gears: 8-speed Shimano Alfine hub gear // Tires: 28" // Brakes: Shimano hydraulic disc brakes
Battery: Bosch Lithium-Ion 36 V 11 Ah 400 Wh // Type of drive: Bosch center motor 250 W
Max. range: 120 mi / 190 km // Speed: 15 mph / 25 km/h // Design: ZEG

HIP-HOP

TYRON RICKETTS ON
E BIKE ADVANCED TECHNOLOGIES GMBH
R004 29ER

Country: Germany
Year: 2013
Weight: 42 lb / 19 kg
Frame: aluminum
Gears: 10-speed Shimano XT precision rear derailleur
Tires: 29"
Brakes: XT premium disc brakes, perforated
Battery: Bosch Lithium-Ion 400 Wh
Type of drive: Bosch center motor 250 W
Max. range: 120 mi / 190 km
Speed: 15 mph / 25 km/h
Design: EBIKE. Das Original

Tyron Ricketts is an all-around media talent. He works as a musician, actor, and TV moderator, and he campaigns against racism and xenophobia. He is a member of Brothers Keepers, a group of artists and producers who creatively oppose discrimination with their music. Through his involvement with Brothers Keepers, this half Jamaican met Harry Belafonte, who now wants to help Tyron make a name for himself in Hollywood. A few years ago, the artist saw his first e-bike at an event held by the Boston Consulting Group. "I took it for a test ride and absolutely loved it. I had ridden bicycles, scooters, and motorcycles my whole life, but e-bikes are something else entirely."

I HAD RIDDEN BICYCLES, SCOOTERS, AND MOTORCYCLES MY WHOLE LIFE, BUT E-BIKES ARE SOMETHING ELSE ENTIRELY.

In the winter of 2012, the 39-year-old rapper moved to Los Angeles not only for work, but also to be near the ocean, since he loves surfing. The only downside of the move is that he couldn't take his e-bike. The battery is considered hazardous because it could implode. "It would have been incredibly expensive to ship my e-bike. Besides, I won't be riding it in LA as much anyway. The distances are too great, and the traffic is just too extreme," he says.

Tyron lived in Berlin for a long time. For him, Berlin is the perfect city for riding an e-bike. It is not as spread out as other big cities, but it is large enough that it would sometimes be too far to ride a normal bike. "The greatest thing about an e-bike is the speed. I'm practically the fastest in the city, apart from the crazy motorcycle riders! I'm faster than bicycles and scooters, definitely faster than pedestrians, and when cars are stuck in a traffic jam, I can simply fly on past and quickly get from point A to point B," explains the musician enthusiastically. He uses his e-bike to ride to work, run errands, or get to practice.

"I was on my way to band practice one time when two guys on a scooter stopped next to me at a red light. Since I ride a scooter too, I know the game, and I challenged them to a race. I knew that with the two of them on the scooter, they would be heavier and slower than me. Of course they didn't take me seriously. Back then I had a different e-bike, a bright red Race R001. On that particular model, the battery is hidden in the frame and you can't tell right away that it's an e-bike. I left them in the dust and then I waited for them at the top of the hill. They were absolutely dumbfounded."

Released in the summer of 2012, Tyron's new album "Weltenreiter" was created during a seven-month trip around the world. Tyron describes his music as melodic rap for adults. His songs are about home, about getting there and making it, and about understanding yourself—definitely not about e-bikes.

Tyron Ricketts ist ein mediales Multitalent. Er arbeitet als Musiker, Schauspieler, TV-Moderator und setzt sich gegen Rassismus und Fremdenhass ein. Er ist Mitglied bei Brothers Keepers, einem Zusammenschluss aus Künstlern und Produzenten, die mit ihrer Musik kreativen Widerstand gegen Diskriminierung leisten. Über sein Engagement dort lernte der Halbjamaikaner Harry Belafonte kennen, der ihm nun helfen will, in Hollywood Fuß zu fassen. Vor ein paar Jahren sah der Künstler bei einer Veranstaltung der Boston Consulting Group das erste Mal ein E-Bike. „Ich bin es Probegefahren und war begeistert. Ich war mein Leben lang mit Fahrrädern, Rollern, Motorrädern unterwegs, aber E-Bikes sind noch mal 'ne andere Nummer."

Der 39-jährige Rapper ist im Winter 2012 nach Los Angeles gezogen, für den Job und auch ein bisschen fürs Meer, denn er liebt das Surfen. Der Wermutstropfen an der Sache: Sein E-Bike konnte er nicht mitnehmen. Der Akku wird als Gefahrentransport definiert, er könnte implodieren. „Der Transport wäre unfassbar teuer. Ganz abgesehen davon, dass ich in L. A. auch nicht so viel fahren würde. Die Strecken sind zu weit, der Verkehr zu krass", sagt er.

Tyron hat lange in Berlin gelebt. Für ihn ist Berlin die perfekte Stadt zum E-Bike-Fahren, nicht so weitläufig wie andere Metropolen, aber doch so groß, dass man manchmal mit einem normalen Rad zu lange unterwegs wäre. „Das Geile am E-Bike ist einfach die Geschwindigkeit. In der Stadt bin ich praktisch der Schnellste, abgesehen von verrückten Motorradfahrern! Schneller als Fahrräder und Roller, schneller als Fußgänger sowieso, und wenn die Autos im Stau stecken, flitze ich einfach vorbei und komm fix von A nach B", schwärmt der Musiker, der sein E-Bike nutzt, um zur Arbeit zu fahren, schnell Besorgungen zu machen oder zum Proberaum zu kommen.

„Ich war auf dem Weg zur Bandprobe, als an der roten Ampel zwei Jungs auf einem Roller neben mir anhielten. Da ich selber auch Roller fahre, kenne ich natürlich das Spielchen und habe sie zum Rennen herausgefordert. Ich wusste, die sitzen zu zweit auf dem Roller, sind also schwer und auf jeden Fall langsamer als ich. Sie haben mich natürlich nicht ernst genommen. Damals hatte ich ein anderes E-Bike, ein feuerrotes Race R001. Bei dem Modell ist der Akku im Rahmen versteckt und man sieht nicht auf den ersten Blick, dass es ein E-Bike ist. Ich bin ihnen also schadenfroh davongefahren und habe dann oben auf dem Berg auf sie gewartet. Die waren total perplex."

Im Sommer 2012 hat Tyron sein neues Album „Weltenreiter" veröffentlicht, das auf einer siebenmonatigen Weltreise entstanden ist. Er beschreibt seine Musik als melodischen Rap für Erwachsene. Es geht um Heimat, ums Ankommen, um die Auseinandersetzung mit sich selbst. Nur um E-Bikes geht es nicht.

A CRANE'S POISE

UTOPIA VELO GMBH // KRANICH

Cross frames have been built since the 1880s and are one of the oldest frame designs. They offer uniform directional stability, give bicycles a particularly high level of solidity and can carry up to 400 pounds. Utopia Velo is a company that recognized the benefits offered by this frame design at an early stage and has spent 25 years on developing its structural engineering. The Kranich is now available as a pedelec with e-support in different frame sizes. Thanks to its step-through frame, the Kranich is an all-round city bike that is popular with women and men alike. Like elegant cranes, the migratory birds that inspired its name, the Kranich is also well-suited for longer rides; riders can quickly attach panniers, a trailer, and a water bottle.

Kreuzrahmen werden seit den 1880er-Jahren gebaut und gehören damit zu den ältesten Rahmenformen. Sie sorgen für einen gleichmäßigen Geradeauslauf, verleihen dem Rad eine besonders hohe Stabilität und können bis zu 180 Kilogramm tragen. Das Haus Utopia Velo erkannte früh die Vorteile dieser Rahmenkonzeption und entwickelt seit nunmehr 25 Jahren seine Bautechnik ständig weiter. Heute ist der Kranich auch als Pedelec mit E-Support und in verschiedenen Rahmengrößen erhältlich. Der Allrounder für die City ist dank des Durchstiegs bei Frauen ebenso beliebt wie bei Männern. Wie sein Namensgeber, der elegante Zugvogel, eignet sich der Kranich aber auch für längere Touren; Taschen, Anhänger und Trinkflasche lassen sich schnell am Rad befestigen.

Country: Germany // Year: 2010 // Weight: 66 lb / 30 kg // Frame: CrMo welded steel

Gears: optional 8-/14-/27-speed, NuVinci // Tires: 26" or 28" // Brakes: Magura HS11 hydraulic rim brakes

Battery: Lithium-Ion cobalt 36 V 12.4 Ah 446.4 Wh (2x) // Type of drive: Utopia E-Support front wheel hub motor 250 W

Max. range: 100 mi / 160 km (with 2 batteries) // Speed: 15 mph / 25 km/h // Design: Utopia Velo GmbH

AWARD-WINNER

GRACE // EASY

The e-bikes from Grace, a high-tech metalworking shop based in Berlin, are no longer an insider secret. The latest example is the purist Grace Easy, an urban bike which won the prestigious Red Dot Award for its design in 2012. Like the Grace Pro, which was introduced by Michael Hecken in a Berlin art gallery in 2009, the Easy picks up on the idea of a fully integrated e-bike concept. Yet the technology is also a sight to behold. Equipped with the nearly indestructible Gates Carbon Drive and state-of-the-art recharging technology, it is the perfect companion for a ride in the urban jungle.

Längst kein Geheimtipp mehr sind die E-Bikes der Hightechschmiede Grace aus Berlin. Jüngstes Beispiel ist das puristische Stadtrad Grace Easy, das für sein Design 2012 den renommierten Red Dot Award abgeräumt hat. Wie schon das 2009 in einer Berliner Kunstgalerie von Michael Hecken vorgestellte Grace Pro greift das Easy hierbei den Gedanken eines voll integrierten E-Bike-Konzepts auf. Aber auch die Technik kann sich sehen lassen. Ausgestattet mit dem nahezu unverwüstlichen Gates Carbon Drive und modernster Rekuperationstechnik, ist es der perfekte Begleiter für den Ausritt im urbanen Dschungel.

Country: Germany // Year: 2013 // Weight: 42 lb / 19 kg // Frame: aluminum // Gears: 3-speed SRAM i-Motion
Tires: 28" // Brakes: Magura MT4 disc brakes // Battery: BionX Lithium-Ion Manganese 48 V 6.3 Ah 303 Wh
Type of drive: BionX IGH 3 rear wheel hub motor 350 W // Max. range: 35 mi / 60 km // Speed: 25 mph / 41 km/h
Design: Andreas Wildgrube

Country: Germany // Year: 2012 // Weight: 57.5 lb / 26.1 kg // Frame: aluminum // Gears: 3-speed gear hub integrated SRAM I-Motion 3
Tires: 26" // Brakes: Magura MT4 hydraulic disc brakes // Battery: BionX Lithium-Ion 48 V 8.4 Ah 403 Wh
Type of drive: BionX rear wheel hub motor 250 W (UK: 200 W / USA: 350 W) // Max. range: 60 mi / 100 km // Speed: 15 mph / 25 km/h
Design: smart Design

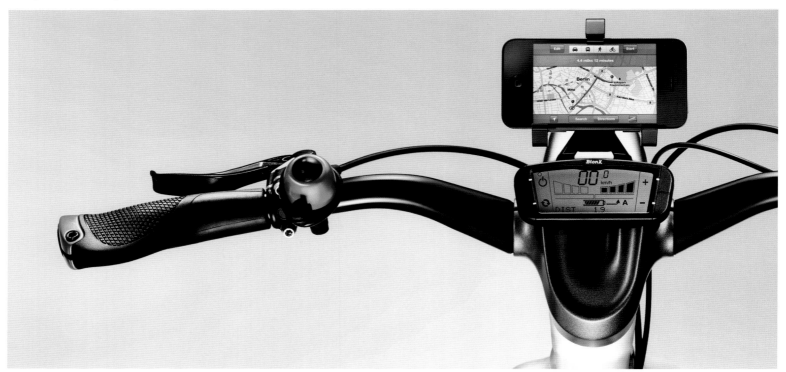

GET SMARTER

SMART // SMART EBIKE

Smart's electric bike needs even less parking space than their zippy small cars and offers some intelligent new details and solutions. A control unit serving as electronic lock and a dock for a smartphone that functions as navigation center—these are only two of the clever features on the the car manufacturer's smart ebike. Remove the control unit from the cradle that's integrated into the handlebars and the drive system is deactivated. The smart ebike recovers power from regenerative braking to recharge the battery, which is smoothly integrated as part of the frame. It also supplies the smartphone with energy via a USB port while you ride. A specially developed app provides the rider with useful additional information.

Benötigen die Stadtflitzer von smart schon wenig Parkraum, geht der Autohersteller mit seinem electric bike noch einen Schritt weiter in Richtung urbane Mobilität. Die Steuer- und Informationszentrale als elektronisches Schloss ist nur eine der schlauen Lösungen des flotten Citymobils. Fehlt die Konsole im Dock am Lenker, ist der Antrieb deaktiviert. Beim Bremsen gewinnt das smart ebike Energie zurück, um den im Rahmen integrierten Akku aufzuladen. Ein Smartphone kann als Navigationssystem sicher am Lenker fixiert werden und erhält während der Fahrt über einen USB-Anschluss Energie. Eine eigene App liefert weitere Informationen und Funktionen.

CITY ELEGANCE

HADI TEHERANI E-BIKE // HADI TEHERANI E-BIKE

Designing a timeless e-bike—that was the goal of star architect Hadi Teherani. His bicycle is both stylish and delicate. One special feature is the detachable handlebar-mounted battery bag, which makes the bicycle and the battery completely independent of each other. Thanks to this feature, the electric support can be upgraded to match the latest developments. Timeless and contemporary, what more could you want?

Ein zeitloses E-Bike zu entwerfen – das war der Wunsch des Stararchitekten Hadi Teherani. Sein Fahrrad präsentiert sich stilvoll und filigran. Eine Besonderheit ist die abnehmbare Akkutasche am Lenker, wodurch Rad und Akku voneinander unabhängig sind. So kann die Elektrounterstützung den aktuellen Entwicklungen am Markt angepasst werden. Zeitlos zeitgemäß, was will man mehr?

Country: Germany // Year: 2011 // Weight: 36 lb / 16,5 kg // Frame: CroMo steel
Gears: 2-speed Sturmey Archer Duomatic hub // Tires: 27" // Brakes: Promaxx special caliper and coaster brakes
Battery: Lithium-Ion 36 V 6.6 Ah 244 Wh // Type of drive: TS comp. Model HLS 1 front wheel hub motor 250 W
Max. range: 25 mi / 40 km // Speed: 15 mph / 25 km/h // Design: Hadi Teherani

THE HAPPY RIDE

ELECTROLYTE // STRASSENFEGER 2

The name says it all, at least when it comes to Beppo, the happy "Straßenfeger" or street sweeper from Michael Ende's book "Momo." Beppo advises us never to think of a strenuous job in its entirety; instead, we should only focus on the very next step. In the same vein, the Straßenfeger 2 is not really suited for the Tour de France. It is not an electric bicycle that boasts about how fast it is or how far it can go. Made by Electrolyte, this model promises nothing more than a great everyday experience. Developed by people who love bicycles, it deliberately avoids technical gimmicks—with the exception of the turbo button on the handlebars for those strenuous uphill climbs.

Der Name ist Programm, zumindest wenn man an den glücklichen Straßenfeger Beppo aus Michael Endes „Momo" denkt. Der erklärt, dass man eine anstrengende Arbeit nie als Ganzes betrachten, sondern sich immer nur auf das jeweils nächste Stück konzentrieren sollte. So hat auch der Straßenfeger 2 gar nicht den Anspruch, bei der Tour de France mitzumischen. Es ist kein Pedelec, das damit prahlt, wie schnell es ist oder wie weit es kommen kann. Das Modell von Electrolyte will nichts weiter, als ein gutes Fahrrad sein. Von Fahrradliebhabern entwickelt, verzichtet es bewusst auf technischen Schnickschnack – abgesehen vom Turboknopf am Lenker für anstrengende Fahrten bergauf.

Country: Germany // Year: 2013 // Weight: starting at 31 lb / 14 kg // Frame: aluminum
Gears: 2-speed Sturmey Archer hub gear // Tires: 28" // Brakes: Series 2013: Magura MT4 disc brakes
Battery: Electrolyte Lithium-Ion 36 V 8.7 Ah 313 Wh // Type of drive: Electrolyte front wheel hub motor 250 W
Max. range: 30 mi / 50 km // Speed: 15 mph / 25 km/h // Design: Matthias Blümel

Country: Germany // Year: 2012 // Weight: 39 lb / 17.8 kg // Frame: Cromoly steel frame, classically lugged // Gears: single speed
Tires: 28" // Brakes: Shimano road-style caliper brake / rim brake // Battery: Panasonic Lithium-Ion 24 V 9 Ah 225 Wh
Type of drive: PB Powerbike rear wheel drive 250 W // Max. range: 30 mi / 45 km // Speed: 15 mph / 25 km/h // Design: Steve Ki

RETRO DREAM

THE URBAN FACTOR // BLACK BEAUTY 2.0

This monochrome marvel is aimed at style-conscious urbanites: ultra-fashionable, yet still offering riders a workout, since it has only a single speed—unless you happen to be the proud owner of a Black Beauty 2.0. This e-bike discretely conceals its battery in a leather bag behind the saddle. A chip controller regulates the amount of electric assistance, while pedaling or riding downhill helps to charge the battery. Each of these classically designed bicycles from the urban factor is made by hand and tested in their Munich bicycle works.

Die Schwarze Schönheit ist für trendbewusste Stadtmenschen gedacht: todschick, aber leider auch schweißtreibend. Denn sie ist ein Singlespeed, das heißt, man hat nur einen Gang zur Verfügung. Außer man ist stolzer Besitzer eines Black Beauty 2.0. Es versteckt seine Batterie dezent in einer Ledertasche hinter dem Sattel. Mittels Chipsteuerung wird die elektronische Unterstützung geregelt. Beim Treten und Bergabfahren lädt sich der Akku zum Teil wieder auf. Jedes der klassisch designten Räder von the urban factor wird auf Bestellung in Handarbeit in der Münchner Radschmiede gefertigt und geprüft.

HIPSTER'S PARADISE

KETTLER // BERLIN ROYAL-E

The Kettler Berlin Royal-e is the ultimate hipster dream. It's almost as if grandma's knit sweater from the '70s came with an integrated iPhone connection. This bike makes its mark with an unaffected retro look: The headlight, the saddle, and the saddle bag feature an endearingly old-fashioned style. Its appearance conveys the sense of being rock solid and almost cozy. Add to that a state-of-the-art lithium-ion battery that deliberately contrasts with the retro design and makes the bike so very exciting. The range of this men's bike is impressive: up to 120 miles.

Das Kettler Berlin Royal-e ist der absolute Hipstertraum. Fast so, als hätte Omas Strickpulli aus den 70ern einen integrierten iPhone-Anschluss. Das Bike überzeugt durch seinen unaffektierten Retrolook: Die Lampe, der Sattel und die Tasche sind liebevoll auf alt getrimmt. Sein Äußeres vermittelt etwas Grundsolides, fast Gemütliches. Dazu kommt eine hochmoderne Lithium-Ionen-Batterie, die im bewussten Kontrast zum Design steht und das Bike so spannend macht. Beeindruckend ist die enorme Ausdauer: Bis zu 190 Kilometer können auf dem Herrenfahrrad zurückgelegt werden.

Country: Germany // Year: 2013 // Weight: 56 lb / 25.4 kg // Frame: aluminum 7005

Gears: 8-speed Shimano Nexus // Tires: 28" // Brakes: Shimano BR-IM81 roller brake

Battery: Bosch Lithium-Ion Manganese 36 V 11 Ah 400 Wh // Type of drive: Bosch center motor 250 W

Max. range: 120 mi / 190 km // Speed: 15 mph / 25 km/h

BAMBOO BOOST

BOO BICYCLES // BOO-T-È-BIONX

The frame of this luxury vehicle is meticulously handmade from bamboo and carbon and tailored to meet the customer's requirements. This e-bike appeals to a wider audience than just environmentally conscious people who value sustainable materials. Technology lovers will appreciate the Boo-T-è-BionX as well: The bamboo-carbon hybrid frame is ultra lightweight, has a higher tensile strength than steel, and is unbreakable and impact-resistant. The hybrid frame has damping properties that are four times higher than those of a 100% carbon frame. Even the rack is strong—designed to hold up to 220 pounds.

Der Rahmen dieses Luxusgefährts wird in akribischer Handarbeit aus Bambus und Carbon gefertigt und den Wünschen des Kunden angepasst. Nicht nur umweltbewusste Menschen, die auf nachhaltige Materialien Wert legen, spricht dieses E-Bike an. Auch Technikbegeisterte kommen beim Boo-T-è-BionX auf ihre Kosten: Der Bambus-Carbon-Hybrid-Rahmen ist ultraleicht, stabiler als Stahl und bruch- und schlagfest. Er verfügt über Dämpfungseigenschaften, die viermal so stark sind wie die bei reinem Carbon. Auch der Gepäckträger hält einiges aus – er trägt bis zu 100 Kilogramm Last.

Country: USA / Vietnam / Switzerland // Year: 2011 // Weight: 39.5 lb / 18 kg // Frame: bamboo-carbon hybrid
Gears: 18-speed Shimano XT // Tires: 18" // Brakes: Shimano XT disc brakes
Battery: BionX Lithium-Ion 48 V 8.8 Ah 423 Wh // Type of drive: BionX PL 250 HT SL XL rear wheel hub motor 250 W
Max. range: 65 mi / 105 km // Speed: 28 mph / 45 km/h // Design: Nick Frey, James Wolf, Daniel Hermann

PIONEER
VÕ THỊ NHUNG ON
ASAMA // A-48

Country: Taiwan
Weight: 104 lb / 47 kg
Frame: forged steel
Tires: 22"
Brakes: front: caliper brakes, rear: drum brakes
Battery: 48 V
Speed: 19 mph / 30 km/h

Võ Thị Nhung is 40 years old. She was born and raised in Tra Vinh City, 125 miles south of Ho Chi Minh City, the capital of Vietnam, which is still known as Saigon outside of the country. The fact that the city was renamed and became the capital of a united North and South Vietnam in 1976 as a result of the Vietnam War seems to have received little notice internationally. Many Vietnamese also continue to use the old name, although strictly speaking "Saigon" is only one district of today's city. Ho Chi Minh City is a name that many find too long and unwieldy.

At age 22, Võ Thị Nhung came to Saigon to marry her husband to whom she is still happily married. Back then, Võ was a designer. Since then she has opened her own bicycle store and discovered e-bikes for herself. All the e-bikes she sells in her store are from Asama, a Taiwanese manufacturer. Her sister also sells electric bicycles and recommended one to her several years ago for environmental reasons. Yet, polluting motorcycles are the primary mode of transportation in Saigon. The entire city is filled with rattling mopeds which are used to transport bulky loads and even entire families. "E-bikes are cheaper than motorcycles," explains Võ, "both in terms of their purchase price as well as their maintenance costs. You don't need gasoline, for example."

Võ rides her e-bike to shop at local markets and for other short trips. "If I have longer distances to travel, I do prefer a motorcycle," says the Vietnamese woman.

THE FIRST TIME I RODE AN E-BIKE, IT ALMOST FELT LIKE RIDING A NORMAL BICYCLE.

"The first time I rode an e-bike, it almost felt like riding a normal bicycle. It was just easier to pedal." Especially because she occasionally rides a motorcycle, she appreciates the fact that e-bikes are not as heavy and are so easy to maneuver.

Võ describes how she used to attract a lot of attention on her e-bike. Even in Saigon with its population of over six million, electric bicycles were something special. People asked her a lot of questions: How far can you ride with it? How long does the battery last? How much does it cost? "Today no one asks me questions anymore," says Võ. Maybe everyone has gotten used to e-bikes, and Võ's pioneering alternative will soon become a popular alternative among Saigon's congested city traffic.

Võ Thị Nhung ist 40 Jahre alt. Geboren und aufgewachsen ist sie in Tra Vinh City, 200 Kilometer südlich von Ho Chi Minh City, der Hauptstadt Vietnams. Der alte Name Saigon wird weltweit noch verwendet. Die Umbenennung der Stadt, die infolge des Vietnamkriegs 1976 zur Hauptstadt vom vereinten Nord- und Südvietnam wurde, hat man international wenig wahrgenommen. Auch viele Vietnamesen sprechen immer noch von Saigon, obwohl das genau genommen nur einen Bezirk der heutigen Stadt bezeichnet. Ho Chi Minh City ist umständlich und lang.

Mit 22 kam Võ Thị Nhung nach Saigon, um zu heiraten. Einen Mann, mit dem sie auch heute noch glücklich zusammenlebt. Damals war Võ Designerin. Inzwischen hat sie ihren eigenen Fahrradladen eröffnet und außerdem das E-Bike für sich entdeckt. Alle E-Bikes, die sie im Angebot hat, stammen von der taiwanesischen Firma Asama. Auch ihre Schwester verkauft Elektroräder und hatte ihr vor einigen Jahren eines empfohlen, aus ökologischen Gründen. Das Haupttransportmittel in Saigon sind dagegen Motorräder. In der ganzen Stadt wimmelt es von knatternden Mopeds, auf denen Waren, sperrige Lasten, ganze Familien transportiert werden. „E-Bikes sind billiger als Motorräder", erklärt Võ, „im Kaufpreis, aber auch bei den Unterhaltskosten. Man braucht zum Beispiel kein Benzin."

Võ fährt mit ihrem E-Bike auf die Märkte zum Einkaufen und nutzt es für kürzere Distanzen. „Wenn ich weite Strecken vor mir habe, nehme ich doch lieber ein Motorrad", sagt die Vietnamesin.

„Als ich das erste Mal auf einem E-Bike saß, hat es sich fast wie auf einem normalen Fahrrad angefühlt. Nur das Treten ist leichter." Gerade weil sie ab und zu auf ein Motorrad steigt, mag sie am E-Bike, dass es nicht so schwer ist und stattdessen sehr wendig.

Võ erzählt, dass sie früher oft auf ihr E-Bike angesprochen wurde. Selbst in Saigon mit seinen über sechs Millionen Einwohnern waren die elektrischen Fahrräder etwas Besonderes. Die Leute fragten sie aus: Wie weit kannst du damit fahren? Wie lang hält die Batterie? Wie viel kostet es? „Heute fragt niemand mehr", sagt Võ. Vielleicht haben sich alle an E-Bikes gewöhnt und die Zeiten, in denen Võ eine Vorreiterin im dichten Stadtverkehr von Saigon war, sind vorbei.

EYE-CATCHER

RALEIGH // DUNDEE ICOMPACT

This new Raleigh is a real eye-catcher. In addition to deep black, this model is also available in flame red and grass green. Even though bold colors tend to be unusual for an electric bike, daring to go with one of these vivid options pays off, as they perfectly set off the geometry of the frame. The short wheelbase and the small wheels make the Dundee iCompact highly maneuverable. The fat tires maintain excellent contact and offer good traction; these, along with the high saddle and sturdy frame, make riders feel as if they're on a mountain bike.

Das neue Raleigh-Bike ist ein richtiger Hingucker. Neben Tiefschwarz ist das Modell auch in Flammenrot und Gras-grün erhältlich. Dabei sind knallige Farben für ein Pedelec eher ungewöhnlich. Doch der Mut zahlt sich aus, denn durch sie wird die Rahmengeometrie perfekt in Szene gesetzt. Der kurze Radstand und die kleinen Räder machen das Dundee iCompact wendig. Die dicken Reifen sorgen für guten Kontakt sowie sicheren Halt und erzeugen – zusammen mit dem hohen Sattel und dem stabilen Rahmen – ein Fahrgefühl wie auf einem Mountainbike.

Country: Germany

Year: 2013

Weight: 45 lb / 20.5 kg

Frame: aluminum

Gears: 8-speed Shimano Nexus

Tires: 20"

Brakes: Magura HS11 Pure QR hydraulic rim brakes

Battery: Impulse Lithium-Ion Compact 36 V 11 Ah 396 Wh

Type of drive: Impulse Pedelec center motor 250 W

Max. range: 85 mi / 135 km

Speed: 15 mph / 25 km/h

Design: Rainer Brinkmann

MAKES YOU SAY "YEAH!"

KREIDLER // VITALITY COMPACT

As a company, Kreidler has achieved many successes with its powered bicycles, mopeds, and lightweight vehicles. It comes as no surprise then that Kreidler has also received top ratings for its Vitality Compact. This small bicycle is a true family vehicle with a saddle and handlebars that can be easily adjusted in a single step, making it easy for both adults and children to ride. Thanks to pedals that can be folded inwards, the Vitality Compact offers a space-saving design and can be easily stowed away. It is equipped with roller brakes and an 8-speed hub gear with a reputation for very low maintenance.

Die Firma Kreidler hat viele Erfolge mit ihren Mofas, Mopeds und Leichtkraftfahrzeugen zu verzeichnen. Kein Wunder also, dass auch das Vitality Compact Bestnoten erzielt. Das Kleinrad ist ein richtiges Familiengefährt: Sattel und Lenker sind mit einem Handgriff verstellbar, sodass es Erwachsene und Kinder gleichermaßen fahren können. Dank seiner einklappbaren Pedale lässt sich das Vitality Compact einfach und platzsparend verstauen. Es verfügt über Rollerbremsen und 8-Gang-Nabenschaltung, die den Ruf haben, wartungsarm zu sein.

Country: Germany // Year: 2013 // Weight: 50 lb / 22.6 kg // Frame: aluminum // Gears: 8-speed Shimano Nexus
Tires: 20" // Brakes: Shimano BR-IM80 roller brakes // Battery: Bosch Lithium-Ion 36 V 8.2 Ah 300 Wh
Type of drive: Bosch center motor 250 W // Max. range: 90 mi / 145 km // Speed: 15 mph / 25 km/h
Design: Rainer Gerdes

WHO WANTS TO BECOME A WINORA RIDER?

WINORA // COMFORT:EXPT

One wheel black, one wheel white—that's stylish! The real highlights, however, are the fully automatic 7-speed Nexus hub gears. Whether heading uphill or handling constant stops and starts in city riding, the automatic gear transmission (AGT) always finds the right gear. If they wish, riders can manually shift gears instead. In either case, thanks to its efficient shifting, the AGT system offers a maximum range of up to 50 miles. It received the Eurobike Award in 2011.

Ein Rad schwarz, ein Rad weiß – stylish! Das eigentliche Highlight ist allerdings die vollautomatisch betriebene Nexus 7-Gang-Nabenschaltung. Ob bei Steigungen oder beim ständigen Anfahren und Abbremsen in der City – die Automatic Gear Transmission, kurz AGT, findet immer den richtigen Gang. Auf Wunsch lässt sie sich auch manuell bedienen. Das AGT-System sorgt in jedem Fall durch effizientes Schaltverhalten für eine maximale Reichweite von bis zu 80 Kilometern. Dafür gab es 2011 den Eurobike Award.

Country: Germany // Year: 2012 // Weight: 61 lb / 27.6 kg // Frame: aluminum

Gears: 7-speed Shimano Nexus, automatic transmission // Tires: 20" // Brakes: Tektro Draco hydraulic disc brakes

Battery: JD/TranzX Lithium-Ion 36 V 11 Ah 396 Wh // Type of drive: Mionic EXP front wheel hub motor 250 W

Max. range: 50 mi / 80 km // Speed: 15 mph / 25 km/h // Design: Felix Puello, Enrico Haase, Karolin Koberstein

LITTLE BLACK HORSE

SOLEX // ESOLEX

The eSolex is the reincarnation of an old cult favorite. Solex, a traditional French company, used to move the masses, helping to get "la grande nation" back on its feet after World War II. The Vélosolex enjoyed many riders, fans, and collectors. Over eight million were produced up until the late 1980s. The reinterpretation of this legendary motorized bicycle has made a two-stroke engine and emissions a thing of the past: The eSolex moves silently with an integrated 400-watt electric motor powered by a powerful lithium-ion battery.

Das eSolex ist die Reinkarnation eines alten Kults. Das französische Traditionsunternehmen Solex bewegte schon früher die Massen und half der Grande Nation nach dem Zweiten Weltkrieg schnell wieder auf die Beine. Das Vélosolex hatte viele Fahrer, Fans und Sammler, über acht Millionen Stück wurden bis in die 80er-Jahre produziert. Die Neuinterpretation des legendären Elektromofas lässt Zweitaktmotor und Emissionen hinter sich: Das eSolex bewegt sich geräuschlos mit einem integrierten 400-Watt-Elektromotor, der von einer starken Lithium-Ionen-Batterie gespeist wird.

Country: France // Year: 2010 // Weight: 101 lb / 46 kg // Frame: aluminum // Gears: single speed
Tires: 20" // Brakes: mechanical disc brakes // Battery: Lithium-Ion Polymer 37 V 16 Ah 592 Wh
Type of drive: rear wheel hub motor 400 W // Max. range: 25 mi / 40 km
Speed: 15 mph / 25 km/h or 22 mph / 35 km/h // Design: Pininfarina

WILD CAT

PANTHERWERKE AG // TE-6K

The comfortable 20-inch TE-6K electric bicycle by Panther is designed for the city. Balloon tires and a HeadShok suspension fork allow this e-bike to take cobblestones and curbs in its stride. Riders will be happy to show off the stylish frame, and the TE-6K even features a rack. The Tektro Auriga disc brakes help keep this wild cat in check—it can even stop on a dime if necessary, since riders can use the power-off function to switch off motor assistance immediately.

Das komfortable 20-Zoll-Pedelec TE-6K von Panther ist für die Stadt gemacht. Dank seiner Ballonreifen und einer dämpfenden HeadShok-Gabel sind Kopfsteinpflaster und Bordsteine keine Hindernisse mehr. Der stylische Rahmen taugt zum Angeben und einen Gepäckträger gibt es auch. Die Tektro-Auriga-Scheibenbremsen halten das Raubtier in Zaum – wenn es sein muss, auch abrupt, denn mit der Power-off-Funktion kann die Motorunterstützung sofort gestoppt werden.

Country: Germany // Year: 2013 // Weight: 46 lb / 21 kg // Frame: aluminum // Gears: 8-speed Shimano Alfine
Tires: 20" // Brakes: Tektro Auriga E-Sub disc brakes with power-off
Battery: Panterra ED3 Lithium-Ion 37 V 8.8 Ah 325 Wh // Type of drive: Panterra Town front wheel hub motor 250 W
Max. range: 50 mi / 80 km // Speed: 15 mph / 25 km/h // Design: Pantherwerke AG

HYBRID RULES!

MARC FEIGENSPAN ON
THIRD ELEMENT // MOTOBIKE

Country: Germany

Year: 2010

Weight: 79 lb / 36 kg

Frame: aluminum tubular frame

Gears: 14-speed Rohloff Speedhub 500/14

Tires: 24"

Brakes: Magura Julie disc brakes

Battery: Clean Mobile Lithium-Ion 48 V 16.8 Ah 840 Wh

Type of drive: Clean Mobile center motor 1,200 W

Max. range: 30 mi / 50 km

Speed: 28 mph / 45 km/h

Design: Third Element

"I'm sticking with hybrid," has become Marc Feigenspan's guiding principle. He has been riding an e-bike for five years noe. Bicycles are this musician and composer's passion. He owns road bikes and mountain bikes, he even owned a bicycle store at one point, and was a bicycle courier in New York City for years. It is perfectly understandable that he was highly curious about hybrid technology involving pedals and batteries. Marc explains the success of e-bikes: "You can reap the benefits of a motor vehicle and still do something for your body and health."

Marc wanted to know what his new vehicle was capable of and wondered: "What is the best test of muscle strength and motor power?" The answer: mountains! He packed his backpack, strapped a video camera onto his helmet, and in the summer of 2012 pedaled over the Alps to Venice. "The harder I pedal, the more power is supplied by the motor. You can think of it as an exercise machine: You give it your all, the motor supports you, and in the end you are exhausted and happy."

PEOPLE HAVE TO LEARN TO RELY MORE ON THEIR EYES WHEN CHECKING TRAFFIC AND NOT JUST DEPEND ON THEIR EARS.

Riding in the city is more difficult. Since e-bikes do not produce engine noise, some passersby are surprised and annoyed by the fast, quiet bicycle. That is why some consideration is being given to equipping e-bikes with engine-like noise. Marc knows a lot about acoustics. As a sound designer, he embellishes movies with music and sounds and knows where he does not want any noise. "People have to learn to rely more on their eyes when checking traffic and not just depend on their ears. It won't take long for them to get used to the fact that there are now vehicles on the road that are fast and quiet." It is the vision of a new modern era: Moving silently through a city where, despite technology and motors, there is no traffic to be heard.

Yet legislation in Germany has not kept pace with e-bike development. "I am not allowed to ride on bike paths because I'm too fast, but I'm not allowed to ride in nature either because I have a motor. I can legally ride on roads, but there I am tailgated and honked at by cars because I'm too slow." However, he still enjoys riding his e-bike: "Legal or not, I'm sticking with hybrid."

„I AM HYBRID", ist zum Leitsatz von Marc Feigenspan geworden, der seit fünf Jahren E-Biker ist. Fahrräder sind die Passion des Musikers und Komponisten. Er besitzt Rennräder und Mountainbikes, sogar ein Fahrradladen hat ihm gehört und er war jahrelang Fahrradkurier in New York City. Nur verständlich, dass seine Neugierde auf die Hybridwesen mit Pedalen und Batterien groß war. Den Erfolg von E-Bikes erklärt Marc so: „Man kann den Vorteil eines Motorfahrzeugs nutzen und tut trotzdem was für seinen Körper und seine Gesundheit."

Marc wollte wissen, was sein neues Gefährt alles kann, und fragte sich: „Was ist der beste Test für Muskelkraft und Motorstärke?" – Berge! Also packte er seinen Rucksack, schnallte sich eine Videokamera auf den Helm und radelte im Sommer 2012 über die Alpen bis nach Venedig. „Je kräftiger ich in die Pedale trete, desto mehr Leistung bringt der Motor. Das kann man sich vorstellen wie einen Hometrainer. Du gibst alles, der Motor unterstützt dich und trotzdem bist du danach ausgepowert und glücklich."

In der Stadt zu fahren ist schwieriger. E-Bikes kündigen sich nicht durch ein Motorengeräusch an und einige Passanten sind überrascht und verärgert über das schnelle, lautlose Rad. Deshalb gibt es Überlegungen, E-Bikes mit motorähnlichen Geräuschen auszustatten. Marc kennt sich mit Tönen aus. Als Sounddesigner gestaltet er Filme mit Musik und Geräuschen aus und weiß, wo er keinen Lärm haben will. „Die Menschen müssen lernen, Verkehr verstärkt über die Augen, nicht nur über die Ohren wahrzunehmen. Sie werden sich daran gewöhnen, dass es jetzt schnelle, leise Fahrzeuge gibt." Es ist die Vision der Moderne: Lautlos durch die Stadt, in der Verkehr nicht mehr zu hören ist, obwohl Technik und Motoren sie bewegen.

Allerdings ist die Gesetzgebung in Deutschland noch nicht so weit entwickelt wie manche E-Bikes. „Ich darf nicht auf Radwegen fahren, weil ich zu schnell bin; in der Natur aber auch nicht, weil ich einen Motor habe. Was legal bleibt, sind die Straßen. Aber hier werde ich von Autos gedrängelt und angehupt, da ich ihnen zu langsam bin." Spaß macht ihm sein E-Bike trotzdem: „Legal ist egal, denn I AM HYBRID."

OFF-ROAD CHAMPION

AVE. HYBRID BIKES // XH7

If there were solar power outlets in the dunes, you could win the Dakar Rally on the XH7. Its knobby tire tread, strong and easily controllable hydraulic disc brakes, 327% gear shifting, and full suspension make for a wild off-road vehicle. Definitely not the kind of bike you would hop on for a casual run to the store! The standard version has a 250-watt Bosch motor and ePower assistance up to 15 miles per hour, and can be upgraded for road traffic. The XH7 Sport special edition comes equipped with a 350-watt motor and offers assistance up to 28 miles per hour, and can only be ridden on private property.

Gäbe es Solarsteckdosen in den Dünen, könnte man mit dem XH7 die Rallye Dakar gewinnen. Dicke Stollen an den Reifen, starke, gut kontrollierbare hydraulische Scheibenbremsen, 327-Prozent-Gangschaltung und eine Voll-federung machen es zu einem wilden Geländefahrzeug. Insgesamt kein Bike, mit dem man mal eben eine Kleinigkeit einkaufen fährt. Die Standardversion mit 250-Watt-Bosch-Motor und ePower-Unterstützung bis 25 Kilometer pro Stunde kann für den Straßenverkehr aufgerüstet werden. Die Sonderedition des XH7 Sport mit 350-Watt-Motor und Unterstützung bis 45 Kilometer pro Stunde darf als Sportgerät ausschließlich auf Privatgelände gefahren werden.

Country: Germany // Year: 2013 // Weight: 49.5 lb / 22.5 kg // Frame: aluminum 6061T6 // Gears: 10-speed 327% Shimano SLX

Tires: 26" // Brakes: Shimano SLX 180 mm hydraulic disc brakes // Battery: Bosch Lithium-Ion 36 V 8 Ah 300 Wh

Type of drive: Bosch center motor 250 W // Max. range: 60 mi / 100 km // Speed: 15 mph / 25 km/h // Design: Stephan Hahn

STREET LEGAL

BULLS GREEN MOVER // E45 OUTLAW

Thanks to its powerful motor, the E45 Outlaw can reach up to 28 miles per hour. Because of its top speed, it needs to be insured and requires a helmet and rearview mirror for riding. For all of these reasons, the bike comes complete with papers and standard certification—even the sheriff shouldn't have any objections. The battery is easy to remove, and its secure housing protects it from the elements.

Das E45 Outlaw kann durch seinen leistungsstarken Motor bis zu 45 Kilometer pro Stunde erreichen. Bei einer solchen Spitzengeschwindigkeit ist das S-Pedelec allerdings auch versicherungspflichtig und darf nur mit Helm und Rückspiegel gefahren werden. Daher wird das Bike inklusive Papieren und Typgenehmigung geliefert. Damit dürfte dann auch der Sheriff keine Einwände haben. Der Akku lässt sich leicht entnehmen und ist durch ein sicheres Gehäuse vor äußeren Einflüssen geschützt.

Country: Germany // Year: 2013 // Weight: 53 lb / 24 kg // Frame: aluminum 7005 // Gears: 30-speed Shimano SLX
Tires: 27.5" // Brakes: Tektro Dorado hydraulic disc brakes // Battery: 10S6P Lithium-Ion 36 V 20.4 Ah 735 Wh
Type of drive: Green Mover rear wheel hub motor 500 W // Max. range: 60 mi / 100 km // Speed: 28 mph / 45 km/h
Design: Atze Etzold, Olaf Thiele

HIGHLANDER

HAIBIKE // XDURO ALL MOUNTAIN

A must-have for off-roaders: The Xduro All Mountain offers 150 mm of suspension travel in the front and 140 mm in the rear, making it ideally equipped to handle uneven terrain. Its maximum ground clearance further protects the motor from rocks. The Haibike features intelligent triple sensor technology which offers fine control of the pedal assistance. The Intuvia on-board computer from Bosch has a separate remote control on the handlebar, which enables riders to adjust the four support modes with just a touch of the thumb—all without having to take their hands off the grip.

Ein Must-have für Offroader: Das Xduro All Mountain bietet 150 Millimeter Federweg vorne und 140 Millimeter hinten und ist somit bestens gewappnet gegen unebenes Gelände. Maximale Bodenfreiheit schützt den Motor außerdem vor Steinschlägen. Das Haibike verfügt über eine intelligente Dreifachsensorik, die eine feingradige Regulierung der Tretunterstützung ermöglicht. Über den Bosch-Bordcomputer „Intuvia" mit separater Fernbedienung am Griff lassen sich die vier Unterstützungsmodi mit dem Daumen einstellen, ohne dass der Fahrer dabei die Hand vom Lenker nehmen muss.

Country: Germany // Year: 2013 // Weight: 46.5 lb / 21,1 kg // Frame: aluminum 606
Gears: 10-speed Shimano Deore XT M 786 Shadow Plus // Tires: 26" // Brakes: Magura MT 4 hydraulic disc brakes
Battery: Lithium-Ion 36 V 11 Ah 400 Wh // Type of drive: Bosch center motor 250 W // Max. range: 120 mi / 190 km
Speed: 15 mph / 25 km/h // Design: Kucher&Thusbass

Country: Germany // Year: 2013 // Weight: 33 lb / 14.9 kg // Frame: aluminum 7005 triple butted // Gears: 30-speed Shimano XT

Tires: 29" // Brakes: Avid Elixir 1 hydraulic disc brakes // Battery: Panasonic Lithium-Ion 36 V 8.6 Ah 310 Wh

Type of drive: Remsdale front wheel hub motor 400 W // Max. range: 30 mi / 50 km // Speed: 18 mph / 30 km/h // Design: Till Rydyger

UPHILL

REMSDALE // 29"

This is the perfect vehicle for passing winded cyclists on a steep mountain grade—while giving them a cheeky grin! Weighing in at just 33 pounds, the Remsdale 29" is one of the lightest electric bicycles around—and that comes in handy when tackling hills. The batteries are invisible from the outside because they are integrated into the lower tubing of the frame.

Es ist das perfekte Gefährt, um hechelnde Radfahrer auf einer Bergetappe zu überholen und ihnen dabei frech ins Gesicht zu grinsen. Mit nur knapp 15 Kilogramm ist das Remsdale 29" eines der leichtesten Pedelecs. Das macht sich natürlich äußerst gut, wenn es bergauf geht. Die Akkus sind von außen nicht sichtbar, da sie im Unterrohr des Rahmens integriert sind.

ROAD RACERS

STEVENS // E-6X DISC

In 1990, brothers Werner and Wolfgang von Hacht founded Stevens, a company based in Hamburg. As former road racers, they know exactly what is important when it comes to sports bicycles. Weighing in at less than 44 pounds, the E-6X is easily powered by muscle strength alone. Once the motor kicks in, three sensors measure pedaling cadence, torque, and speed. This data is then used to calculate how much extra energy the rider requires at any given time. The ergonomic cockpit offers a comfortable sitting position, and the Suntour suspension fork easily smooths out the ride if things get bumpy.

Die Brüder Werner und Wolfgang von Hacht gründeten 1990 das Unternehmen Stevens in Hamburg. Als ehemalige Straßenrennfahrer wissen sie genau, worauf es bei Sporträdern ankommt. Das E-6X wiegt nicht einmal 20 Kilogramm und lässt sich aus diesem Grund auch ausschließlich mit Muskelkraft noch wunderbar bewegen. Summt der Motor, liefern drei Sensoren Messdaten zu Trittfrequenz, Drehmoment und Geschwindigkeit, mit denen errechnet wird, wie viel Extraenergie der Fahrer zu einem bestimmten Zeitpunkt benötigt. Das ergonomische Cockpit sorgt für eine angenehme Sitzposition, und wenn es doch einmal holprig wird, dämpft die Suntour-Federgabel gut ab.

Country: Germany // Year: 2011 // Weight: 44 lb / 19.9 kg // Frame: aluminum 6061DB Superlite // Gears: 10-speed Shimano Deore Shadow
Tires: 28" // Brakes: Shimano BR-M446 hydraulic disc brakes // Battery: Bosch PowerPack 36 V 11 Ah 400 Wh
Type of drive: Bosch center motor 250 W // Max. range: 120 mi / 190 km // Speed: 15 mph / 25 km/h // Design: Volker Dohrmann

OLYMPIC SPIRIT

MARTIN BRAXENTHALER ON OTTO BOCK HEALTHCARE GMBH EMANO HANDBIKE

Country: Germany // Frame: aluminum // Gears: 8-speed Shimano // Tires: 26" // Brakes: Magura disc brakes
Battery: Bosch Lithium-Ion // Type of drive: Bosch // Max. range: 120 mi / 190 km // Speed: 15 mph / 25 km/h

Martin Braxenthaler is one of the most successful paralympians in Germany. In 1994 he had an accident at work. Rocks fell onto his back and he has been a paraplegic ever since. With his disability, Martin changed course from being a decent recreational skier to one of the best monoskiers in the world. If he put all the medals he has won around his neck, he would probably find it difficult to move. At the Paralympic Winter Games held in Vancouver in 2010, for example, he won Gold medals in Super-Combined, Giant Slalom, and Slalom, as well as a Silver medal in Super-G.

As a competitive athlete, Martin has to train year round, even when there is no snow. The handbike has been part of his training program for 16 years—for his conditioning and for his arm muscles. With a handbike, you crank with your arms instead of pedaling with your legs.

Martin has used many handbikes to explore the area surrounding his home, which is located in the alpine foothills near Traunstein. His latest model, the emano handbike by Otto Bock, features electrical assistance. "As a high-performance athlete, I love to push my limits and rely on my own strength. I was skeptical for a long time when it came to bicycles with electrical assistance," recalls this native of Upper Bavaria. Then he tried out a handbike with electrical assistance at a trade show. He was very impressed—even after just a few yards. "It opened up entirely new horizons for me. As a handcyclist you do great if you're riding by yourself, but it is difficult if you want to ride alongside people on regular bicycles. The strength ratio between my arms and their legs is simply very different, and that's noticeable as soon as you start going up a hill. Even handcyclists in good condition wear out quickly in such situations. With electrical assistance, I have more stamina and can go on longer mountain rides with cyclists, without collapsing at some point."

Martin played a significant role in the development of the emano handbike. Some of the features on the bike bear his name and his signature. He has collaborated with Otto Bock's company for some time now on ideas for helping people with physical disabilities achieve the greatest

Martin Braxenthaler ist einer der erfolgreichsten Paralympioniken in Deutschland. 1994 fielen ihm bei einem Arbeitsunfall Steine auf den Rücken, seitdem ist er querschnittsgelähmt. Mit seiner Behinderung entwickelte er sich von einem guten Freizeitskifahrer zu einem der besten Monoskifahrer der Welt. Würde er sich alle gewonnenen Medaillen umhängen, könnte er sich wohl kaum noch bewegen. Allein bei den Paralympischen Winterspielen 2010 in Vancouver gewann er Gold in Superkombi, Riesenslalom, Slalom und Silber in Super-G.

Als Leistungssportler muss er auch während der schneefreien Jahreszeiten trainieren. Das Handbike gehört seit 16 Jahren zu seinem Trainingsprogramm – für die Kondition und für die Armmuskulatur. Anstatt mit den Beinen zu treten, kurbelt man beim Handbike mit den Armen.

Martin ist schon mit vielen Handbikes durch seine Heimat, das Voralpenland bei Traunstein, gekurbelt. Sein neuestes Modell ist das Handbike emano von Otto Bock mit elektronischer Unterstützung. „Als Leistungssportler liebe ich es, mich richtig auszupowern und mich auf meine eigene Körperkraft zu verlassen. Deswegen war ich auch lange skeptisch, was elektronische Unterstützung bei Fahrrädern angeht", erinnert sich der Oberbayer. Dann probierte er ein Handbike mit Antriebshilfe auf einer Messe aus und war nach wenigen Metern schwer beeindruckt. „Da haben sich für mich neue Horizonte eröffnet. Als Handbiker kann man wunderbar alleine fahren, aber mit Radfahrern unterwegs zu sein ist schwierig. Das Kraftverhältnis zwischen meinen Armen und deren Beinen ist einfach sehr unterschiedlich. Sobald es bergauf geht, macht sich das bemerkbar. Selbst Handbiker mit guter Kondition verlieren da schnell viel Kraft. Mit E-Unterstützung bin ich ausdauernder und kann längere Touren mit Radfahrern in den Bergen fahren, ohne dass ich zwischendurch kollabiere."

Martin war maßgeblich an der Entwicklung des emano-Handbikes beteiligt. Einige Features an dem Rad tragen seinen Namen und seine Handschrift. Zusammen mit der Firma Otto Bock entwickelt er schon seit Längerem Ideen, wie man Menschen mit körperlicher Behinderung

possible mobility and quality of life. "Otto Bock realized pretty quickly that I am a practical person who is very familiar with technology. That is why people often get me involved in the development of new products. The same holds true with the bikes."

At this point, the focus of conversation expands from just sports to also to include his desire to involve and integrate the general population of people with handicaps. "There are many people with disabilities who would like to go on bicycle rides," reports Martin, who is a strong proponent for including the disabled. "Many don't dare to try it because they don't have enough strength in their arms and because they are concerned that as soon as they encounter a hill they will be left behind. Electrical assistance represents a tremendous opportunity for people with disabilities to get into handbikes and become active."

I LOVE TO PUSH MY LIMITS.

The winter sports athlete points out that his country is dotted with mountains and hills that would quickly become tests of strength as well as obstacles. "If you think Germany is flat, you need to open your eyes. Sure, 10,000-foot peaks aren't the norm, but if you think you can leave home and ride 30 miles in any direction on level roads without ever encountering a hill—well, you'll find that hard to do."

The athlete points out that riding a handbike is about three times as strenuous as riding a bicycle. "It is a constant strain on your arms! Without assistance, you might make it about 20 to 25 miles. That's only about 10 miles in any direction, so you won't get too far."

The emano handbike expands this radius, making it possible to go on longer rides with friends; it is also enjoyable and enhances one's quality of life. "We are trying to appeal to a group that hasn't dared to try out handbikes until now." But it's about more than just recreation. According to Martin, people with disabilities have to be more aware of their fitness levels. "Particularly for paraplegics or those with other mobility restrictions, they have to move to ensure that their circulatory system, metabolism, and blood flow don't decrease."

In his case, Martin not only uses his e-bike for training, but also to go on rides with his friends and his family. "I simply take off, just like I used to before my accident."

Plans are in the works to integrate a minimalist wheelchair into the bike. That would make users completely mobile, because so far the bike has had a fairly large turning radius. One time, in fact, Martin had maneuvered himself into a place that he couldn't get out of on his own. He asked an elderly couple for help. The husband remarked: "Why don't you just stand up and turn your bike around? You don't need us to do that!" Martin smiled as he recalled the incident. "He simply didn't realize that I am actually a wheelchair user. He felt absolutely terrible when he found out." The e-biker continues: "Most pedestrians are astonished. Bicycle enthusiasts are full of admiration, whereas kids are simply enthusiastic."

zur größtmöglichen Mobilität und Lebensqualität verhelfen kann. „Otto Bock hat ziemlich schnell gemerkt, dass ich ein Praktiker bin, der sich gut auskennt mit Technik. Deshalb bindet man mich oft in die Entwicklung neuer Produkte ein. Und das war bei den Bikes genauso."

Hier überschneidet sich das Thema Sport mit dem Wunsch, Menschen mit Handicap einzubeziehen und zu integrieren. „Es gibt viele bewegungseingeschränkte Menschen, die sich wünschen, Radtouren zu fahren", berichtet Martin, der sich stark für die Inklusion von Behinderten einsetzt. „Viele trauen sich das aber nicht zu, weil sie zu wenig Kraft in den Armen haben, weil sie Bedenken haben, dass sie außen vor bleiben werden, sobald ein Hügel auf der Strecke ist. Die Elektrounterstützung ist eine Riesenchance, ins Handbiken einzusteigen und Sport zu treiben."

Der Wintersportler verweist darauf, dass überall im Land Berge und hüglige Landschaften seien, die schnell zu Kraftproben und Hindernissen würden. „Wer meint, Deutschland sei flach, sollte mal die Augen aufmachen. Klar ist das Land nicht von Dreitausendern bedeckt, aber wenn einer behauptet, er kann von zu Hause aus losfahren, 50 Kilometer in jede Richtung auf ebenen Straßen, ohne auf eine Steigung zu treffen – dem glaub ich erst mal nicht."

Handbiken sei ungefähr dreimal so anstrengend wie Fahrradfahren, vergleicht der Leistungssportler. „Es ist eine Daueranstrengung für die Arme! Ohne Unterstützung schafft man vielleicht gut 30–40 Kilometer. Das sind dann nur rund 15 Kilometer in eine Richtung, da kommt man nicht weit."

Das emano-Handbike erweitert den Radius, längere Touren mit Freunden in der Natur werden möglich, das schenkt Freude und Lebensqualität. „Wir versuchen damit eine Gruppe anzusprechen, die sich bisher das Handbiken nicht zugetraut hat." Aber es geht um mehr als eine Freizeitbeschäftigung. Menschen mit Behinderung, so Martin, müssen sich besonders stark um ihre Fitness kümmern: „Gerade bei Querschnittslähmung oder anderen Mobilitätseinschränkungen muss man sich bewegen, damit das Kreislaufsystem, der Stoffwechsel und die Durchblutung nicht nachlassen."

Martin selbst nutzt das E-Bike nicht nur als Trainingsgerät, sondern auch, um mit seinen Freunden und seiner Familie Radtouren zu machen: „Einfach losfahren, so wie früher, vor meiner Behinderung."

Es wird geplant, in das Bike einen minimalistischen Rollstuhl zu integrieren. Damit wären die Nutzer vollkommen mobil, denn das Bike hat bisher einen ziemlich großen Wendekreis. Einmal hatte sich Martin so ungünstig einrangiert, dass er alleine nicht mehr vom Fleck gekommen ist. Er bat ein älteres Ehepaar um Hilfe. Der Mann meinte: „Steh halt auf und dreh dein Radl um. Da brauchst du uns ja nicht dazu!" Martin kann darüber schmunzeln. „Er hat gar nicht begriffen, dass ich eigentlich Rollstuhlfahrer bin. Natürlich tat es ihm schrecklich leid. Die breite Masse der Fußgänger reagiert mit Verwunderung", schildert der E-Biker, „die Kenner der Bike-Szene mit Bewunderung und die Kinder mit Begeisterung."

Country: Germany // Year: 2010 // Weight: 42 lb / 19 kg // Frame: aluminum superlight EPO Urban Triple Butted // Gears: 30-speed Shimano
Tires: 28″ // Brakes: Shimano hydraulic disc brakes (180/180) // Battery: Aero Seatpost Lithium-Ion 36 V 8.8 Ah 317 Wh
Type of drive: GO SwissDrive rear wheel hub motor 250 W // Max. range: 60 mi / 100 km // Speed: 15 mph / 25 km/h

SLEEK AND SPORTY

CUBE BIKES // EPO NATURE

When it comes to electric bikes it is rare to find a design as elegant and clean as this one. The combination of black lacquer and metallic blue accents makes the Epo a truly elegant beauty. The battery packs are stylishly integrated into the aerodynamic saddle supports and can be charged while on the bike or removed and charged elsewhere. Pinhead locks for the battery, motor, and wheels protect this gem from theft. The control unit is easy to remove when parking or storing the bike. Multi Feature Dropout makes it a snap to add fenders, rack, and kickstand.

So ein elegantes und sauberes Design ist bei Pedelecs eher selten. Die Kombination aus schwarzem Lack und metallicblauen Akzenten macht das Epo zu einer eleganten Schönheit. Dafür sorgen auch die Akkupacks, die geschickt in der aerodynamischen Sattelstütze integriert sind und intern als auch extern geladen werden können. Pinhead-Schlösser für Akku, Motor und Laufräder schützen das Prachtstück vor Diebstahl. Auch die Steuereinheit kann beim Verlassen des Rades einfach abgenommen werden. Und das Multi-Feature-Dropout ermöglicht die einfache Montage von Schutzblech, Gepäckträger und Ständer.

HAVING IT ALL

GIANT // ROAM XR HYBRID

This sporty cross-bike is a true all-purpose vehicle and can be used both in the city and in the country. One special feature is the LCD display, currently the flattest on the market. It is operated using controls on the left handlebar grip. The advantage to this design is that riders don't need to let go of the grip to make adjustments while they're riding over hill and dale. The lithium-ion batteries are mounted for optimal weight distribution. They are removable and lockable and have a range of up to 50 miles. The LED display indicates the charge status of the batteries.

Dieses sportive Crossbike ist ein Allrounder – sowohl innerhalb als auch außerhalb der Stadt einsetzbar. Ein besonderes Highlight ist das LCD-Display, derzeit eines der flachsten am Markt. Es wird über Bedienelemente am linken Lenkergriff gesteuert. Dies bietet den Vorteil, nicht den Griff loslassen zu müssen, wenn es über Stock und Stein geht. Die Lithium-Ionen-Akkus sind so angebracht, dass sich ihr Gewicht optimal verteilt. Sie sind abnehm- und abschließbar und halten bis zu 80 Kilometer. Wie fit die Akkus noch sind, lässt die LED-Ladestandsanzeige erkennen.

Country: Taiwan // Year: 2012/13 // Weight: 49 lb / 22.4 kg // Frame: Giant AluxX aluminum
Gears: 27-speed Shimano Deore shifter // Tires: 28" // Brakes: Shimano M395 disc brakes
Battery: Sanyo Lithium-Ion 36 V 10 Ah 360 Wh // Type of drive: SyncDrive R rear wheel hub motor 250 W
Max. range: 50 mi / 80 km // Speed: 15 mph / 25 km/h // Design: Giant Hybrid Design Team

DIVINE POWER

HERCULES // SPORT PRO

As demonstrated with this all-terrain e-bike, Hercules is a company that believes in regeneration—in other words, the energy that is generated during braking or downhill riding is fed back into the battery. The battery is securely concealed in the main tube, a location that provides it with ideal protection from the weather and from rocks being kicked up from the road. Its weight is the real highlight; at 51.6 pounds, the Sport Pro is astonishingly lightweight for an electric bicycle.

Die Firma Hercules setzt bei ihrem geländetauglichen E-Bike auf Rekuperation, das heißt, die Energie, die beim Bremsen oder Bergabfahren entsteht, wird wieder in den Akku zurückgeführt. Dieser sitzt sicher und gut versteckt im Hauptrohr und ist dadurch bestens vor Wetter und Steinschlägen geschützt. Highlight ist das Gewicht, denn mit 23,4 Kilogramm ist das Sport Pro für ein Pedelec verblüffend leicht.

Country: Germany // Year: 2013 // Weight: 51.5 lb / 23,4 kg // Frame: Alu 6061 P.G.

Gears: 9-speed Shimano Deore XT derailleur // Tires: 28" // Brakes: Shimano XT hydraulic disc brakes

Battery: ION Lithium-Ion 36 V 10 Ah 360 Wh // Type of drive: ION rear wheel hub motor 250 W

Max. range: 60 mi / 100 km // Speed: 15 mph / 25 km/h // Design: Hercules

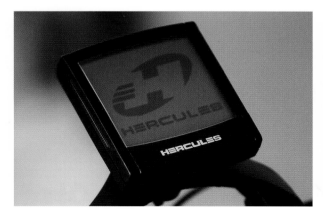

THE PHANTOM

GHOST // E-HYBRIDE TRAIL 9000

Mountain bikes have always been something to boast about, and the Ghost E-Hybride Trail 9000 makes it particularly easy for proud owners to do so: This mountain bike with electric assistance features a chic design and offers plenty of comfort. The powerful battery which supplies power to the 250-watt rear wheel hub motor is concealed in the substantial lower tube of the aluminum frame. The Racing Ralph tires from Schwalbe and the Fox suspension fork ensure that riders can negotiate uneven terrain effortlessly.

Mountainbikes waren schon immer gut zum Prahlen. Und mit dem Ghost E-Hybride Trail 9000 fällt das sichtlich leicht: Das Mountainbike mit Elektrounterstützung überzeugt durch sein schickes Design und seinen Komfort. Ein kraftvoller Akku, der den 250-Watt-Hinterradnabenmotor speist, ist im massiven Unterrohr des Alurahmens versteckt. Die Racing-Ralph-Reifen von Schwalbe und die Fox-Federgabel sorgen dafür, dass der Fahrer auch unebenes Gelände mühelos passieren kann.

Country: Germany // Year: 2013 // Weight: 49 lb / 22.4 kg // Frame: aluminum // Gears: 27-speed Shimano XT // Tires: 26"
Brakes: Shimano XT disc brakes // Battery: ION Lithium-Ion 36 V 10 Ah 360 Wh // Type of drive: ION rear wheel hub motor 250 W
Max. range: 60 mi / 100 km // Speed: 15 mph / 25 km/h // Design: Ghost-Bikes

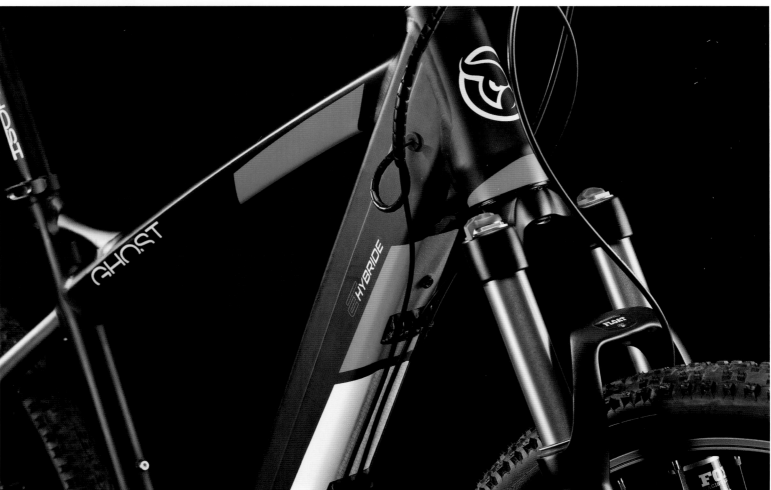

LIGHTNING FAST

STEALTH ELECTRIC BIKES // STEALTH'S BOMBER WHITE

The Stealth Bomber looks like a downhill bike on steroids. Extra-long suspension travel emphasizes the extreme character of this powerful electric bike. With his Stealth e-bikes, company founder John Karabalis goes beyond the conventional bike categories. The weight of the hub motor in the rear wheel improves this downhill bike's traction even more. In competition mode, the Bomber's brushless e-motor manages up to 4,500 watts and, with the aid of a 9-speed transmission, pushes the 117-pound bike to a maximum speed of 50 miles per hour.

Das Stealth Bomber wirkt wie ein Downhill-Bike auf Steroiden. Immense Federwege unterstreichen den extremen Charakter des kraftvollen Elektro-Bikes. Firmengründer John Karabalis sieht sich mit seinen Stealth-E-Bikes außerhalb herkömmlicher Bike-Klassen. Der Nabenmotor im Hinterrad verbessert durch sein Gewicht noch die Traktion im Downhill. Der bürstenlose E-Motor des Bombers leitet im Competition Mode bis zu 4.500 Watt und treibt das 53-Kilo-Bike über ein 9-Gang-Getriebe zu einer Höchstgeschwindigkeit von 80 Stundenkilometern.

Country: Australia // Year: 2012 // Weight: 117 lb / 53 kg // Frame: CrMo alloys
Gears: 9-speed // Tires: 24" // Brakes: Magura MT2 // Battery: Stealth Battery LiFePO4 1,500 Wh
Type of drive: Stealth rear wheel hub motor 4,500-watts brushless DC // Max. range: 50 mi / 80 km
Speed: 50 mph / 80 km/h // Design: John Karabalis

THE CULTIVATED CLASSIC

M55 BIKE // TERMINUS—CLASSIC EDITION

With a limited edition of just 275, this luxury bike truly is something special. The Classic edition is the result of a grand total of six years of work: The frame is manufactured from 7075 aluminum, a material frequently used in aviation. It is milled from a single block; the lack of welded seams makes the frame particularly strong. The electronics, the motor, and the battery packs are all handcrafted. With the Classic models, even the size and weight of the customer is taken into account when some of the components are manufactured and installed. Custom versions made of titanium are also available. Thanks to the maximum attention to detail, this bike makes its rider the winner of every race.

Mit einer limitierten Auflage von 275 Stück ist dieses Luxusbike etwas ganz Besonderes. Die Classic Edition ist die Essenz einer sechsjährigen Arbeit: Der Rahmen ist aus 7075-Aluminium gefertigt, einem Material, das viel in der Luftfahrt zum Einsatz kommt. Es wird aus einem Metallblock gefräst, sodass keine Schweißnähte entstehen, was den Rahmen besonders stark macht. Die Elektronik, der Motor und die Batteriepacks sind handgefertigt. Selbst bei den Classic-Modellen werden einige Bauteile unter Berücksichtigung der Größe und des Gewichts des Kunden hergestellt und eingebaut. Sonderanfertigungen aus Titan sind ebenfalls erhältlich. Bis ins letzte Detail durchdacht, lässt das Bike seinen Fahrer aus jedem Rennen als Sieger hervorgehen.

Country: Hungary

Year: 2011

Weight: 68 lb / 31 kg

Frame: 7075 grade CNC machined aluminum or grade 5 titanium

Gears: 14-speed Rohloff Speedhub

Tires: 26"

Brakes: Hope Tech V2 EVO disc brakes

Battery: Panasonic 18650 43.2 V 37.2 Ah 1,320 Wh

Type of drive: M55 Bike brushless center motor 2,000 W

Max. range: 60 mi / 100 km

Speed: 47 mph / 75 km/h

Design: Richard Szollosi & Peter Szalva

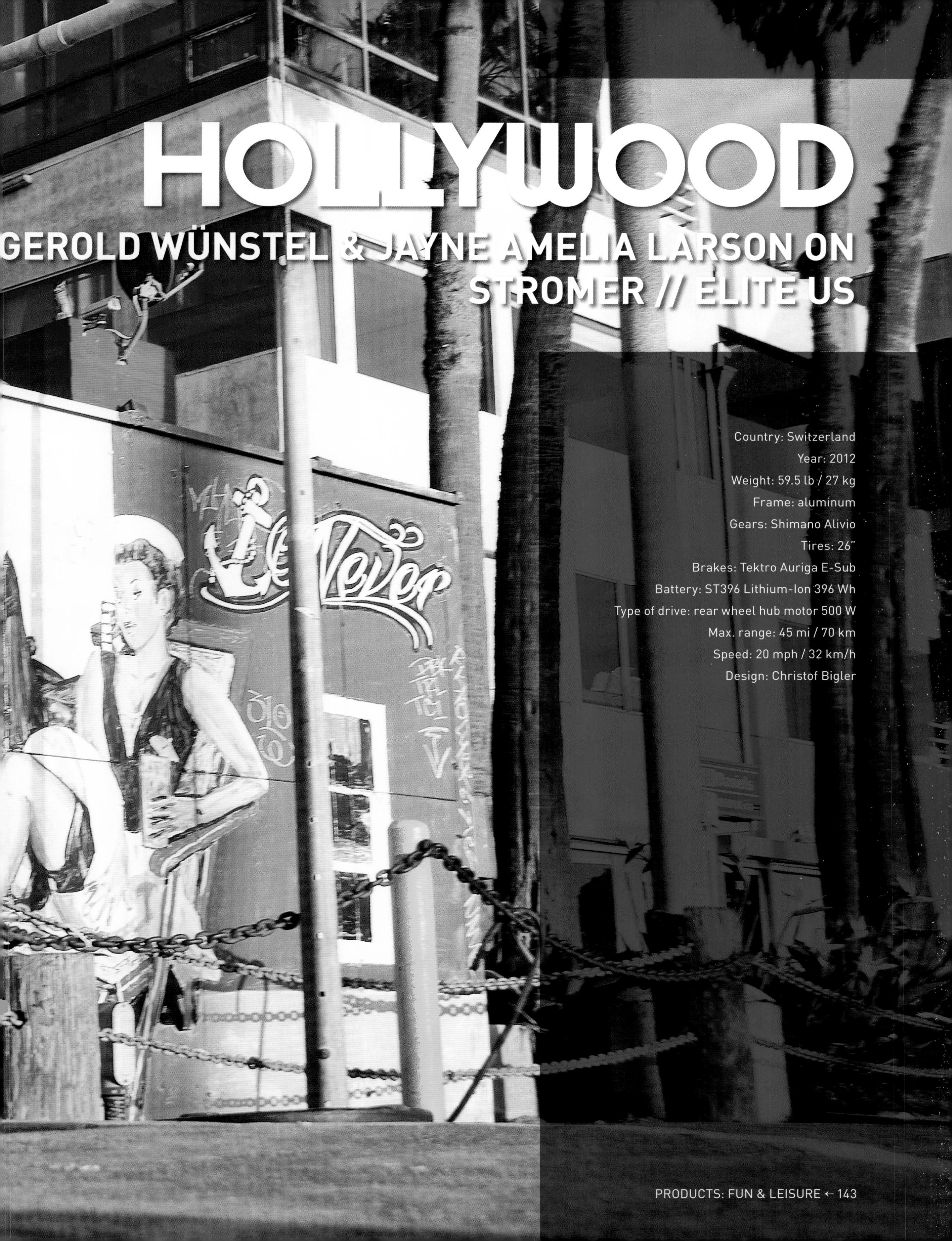

HOLLYWOOD

GEROLD WÜNSTEL & JAYNE AMELIA LARSON ON STROMER // ELITE US

Country: Switzerland
Year: 2012
Weight: 59.5 lb / 27 kg
Frame: aluminum
Gears: Shimano Alivio
Tires: 26"
Brakes: Tektro Auriga E-Sub
Battery: ST396 Lithium-Ion 396 Wh
Type of drive: rear wheel hub motor 500 W
Max. range: 45 mi / 70 km
Speed: 20 mph / 32 km/h
Design: Christof Bigler

Gerold Wünstel is a German-American who has been living in Los Angeles for ten years and describes himself as a "modern nomad." For over 20 years, he worked as a chauffeur in Berlin, New York, San Francisco, and Los Angeles. Gerold embodied the spirit of Scorsese's "Mean Streets" as he safely transported VIPs through the city in his work as a private driver for Hollywood celebrities and as a chauffeur and bodyguard for politicians. Yet two years ago he finally had his fill of cars and started looking for an alternative.

CAR-SHARING WAS NOT THE SOLUTION.

Gerold wanted to escape the stress as well as the increasingly crazy traffic in Los Angeles. Car-sharing was not the solution. He bought himself a brand new red Vespa, on which he planned to weave through the throngs of cars and avoid LA's constant congestion. Bad move! Even on the Vespa he continued to encounter aggressive and erratic drivers, sending his blood pressure sky high.

What to do? Gerold sold his Vespa after three months and moved on to a brand new bicycle with the promising name "Simple City." Yet that was not a satisfactory solution either. Expecting to conquer the traffic on a bicycle in a congested metropolitan area with a population of approximately twelve million is about as hopeless as Don Quixote battling against windmills.

Buses, subway, and light rail offered another option. What? Somebody using public transportation in LA? Actually, this option is not as bad as most tourists or LA residents think. To some degree, using mass transit to get around the city is doable, although not always.

Then, finally, salvation... Through a lucky twist of fate, the e-bike, also known as Pedelec in Germany, entered Gerold's life when he saw his first one at Venice Beach. After a bit of research, he became the proud owner of a modular e-bike made by the Swiss manufacturer Stromer—in a small town in the Bernese Oberland. From that point on, things started to look up: low costs, no gas, no taxes, no insurance, and also an easy conscience because of the e-bike's modest CO_2 footprint. These are just some of its many benefits. Best of all, it is a lot of fun to ride, Gerold feels great mentally, and he doesn't have to worry about joining a gym anymore.

Gerold now rides his e-bike almost every day, often alongside his partner Jayne Amelia Larson. The two have been working as film producers and screenwriters for a while now. Like Gerold, Jayne gave up her job as a chauffeur and no longer drives a car. She describes the bizarre experiences of her former occupation chauffeuring Hollywood celebrities, the super rich, and Saudi princesses in her book "Driving the Saudis," which immediately made the "New York Times" Best Sellers list. Gerold is the co-author and co-producer of the movie "Who Killed Johnny," which is scheduled for a 2013 release in Swiss movie theaters.

Gerold Wünstel ist Deutschamerikaner. Seit zehn Jahren wohnt er in Los Angeles und bezeichnet sich als „moderner Nomade". Er arbeitete über 20 Jahre als Chauffeur in Berlin, New York, San Francisco und Los Angeles. Der Spirit des Martin-Scorsese-Films „Mean Streets" begleitete ihn, während er als Privatchauffeur der Hollywood-Prominenz und als Sicherheitschauffeur von Politikern die VIPs sicher durch die Stadt brachte. Doch vor zwei Jahren hatte er genug vom Automobil und machte sich auf die Suche nach einer Alternative.

Gerold wollte raus aus dem Stress, raus aus dem zunehmenden, irren Straßenverkehr der Megalopolis Los Angeles. Carsharing war keine Lösung. Er kaufte sich eine nagelneue rote Vespa, mit der er sich an den Automassen vorbeischlängeln wollte, um dem ständigen Stau von L. A. zu entgehen. Fehlanzeige. Er war immer noch der täglichen Aggression mit steigendem Puls, zu hohem Blutdruck und bizarren Fahrmanövern ausgesetzt.

Doch was tun? Seine Vespa verkaufte Gerold nach drei Monaten wieder und stieg um auf ein neu erstandenes Fahrrad mit dem vielversprechenden Namen „Simple City". Aber auch das war keine endgültige Lösung. Den Verkehr eines Ballungsgebiets mit rund zwölf Millionen Einwohnern auf dem Fahrrad bezwingen zu wollen ist fast so aussichtslos wie der Kampf von Don Quixote gegen die Windmühlen.

Eine weitere Option boten öffentliche Verkehrsmittel: Busse, U-Bahn oder S-Bahn. Wie bitte? – Ja, genau. Sie sind nicht ganz so schlimm, wie die meisten Touristen oder Angelenos denken. Teilweise ist das Vorhaben, sich per öffentlichem Nahverkehr durch die Stadt zu bewegen, auch durchführbar, aber nicht immer.

Dann endlich die Erlösung: Das E-Bike, in Deutschland auch Pedelec genannt, kam durch eine glückliche Fügung in Gerolds Leben. Am Strand von Venice Beach sieht er zum ersten Mal ein Elektrorad. Nach einigen Recherchen ist er stolzer Besitzer eines modularen E-Bikes der Marke Stromer. Hergestellt in der Schweiz, in einem kleinen Ort im Berner Oberland. Von da an ging's wieder bergauf: geringe Kosten, kein Benzin, keine Steuer, keine Versicherung, stattdessen ein gutes Gewissen wegen eines vertretbaren CO_2-Fußabdrucks. Alles spricht für das E-Bike. Doch das Beste: Es macht enorm viel Spaß, Gerold fühlt sich mental gut und das Fitnessstudio kann er sich jetzt auch sparen.

Inzwischen benutzt er sein E-Bike fast täglich. Öfter auch zusammen mit seiner Partnerin Jayne Amelia Larson. Seit einiger Zeit arbeiten beide nun schon als Filmproduzenten und Drehbuchautoren. Denn auch Jayne hat ihre Tätigkeit als Chauffeurin an den Nagel gehängt und fährt nicht mehr Auto. Die skurrilen Erlebnisse ihres früheren Jobs zwischen Hollywood-Prominenz, Superreichen und saudischen Prinzessinnen beschreibt sie in dem Buch „Driving the Saudis", das es auf Anhieb auf die Bestsellerliste der „New York Times" geschafft hat. Gerold ist Co-Autor und Co-Produzent des Films „Who killed Johnny", der 2013 in den Schweizer Kinos anlaufen soll.

TO THE MOON AND BACK

EROCKIT GMBH // EROCKIT

Berlin-based eRockit GmbH has developed an electric bicycle for superheroes with purchasing power. The eRockit abounds with testosterone-fueled exuberance—on the part of the designers and purchasers alike. Boasting a speed of 50 miles an hour and a maximum torque of 55 pound-force feet, the eRockit is anything but inconspicuous. When it comes down to it, the eRockit doesn't really fit into the speed pedelec category. It's almost a light motorcycle—one that triggers a yearning to hit Route 66. When operated with a combination of power and muscle strength, the bike can cover distances of up to 45 miles.

Die Berliner eRockit GmbH hat ein Pedelec für kaufkräftige Superhelden entwickelt. Das eRockit strotzt vor testosteronbedingtem Übermut – aufseiten der Käufer und der Designer. 81 Kilometer pro Stunde und ein maximales Drehmoment von 75 Newtonmetern – dezent sieht anders aus. Im Grunde kann man das eRockit nicht einmal mehr zu den S-Pedelecs zählen. Es ist vielmehr ein Leichtkraftrad, fast ein Motorrad, das Sehnsucht nach der Route 66 weckt. Mit Strom und Muskelkraft betrieben, lassen sich mit dem Bike Strecken von bis zu 70 Kilometern zurücklegen.

Country: Germany // Year: 2012 // Weight: 271 lb / 123 kg // Frame: aluminum // Gears: 3 electronic speed levels (bicycle mode, standard, fast)
Tires: 18" // Brakes: motorcycle disc brakes // Battery: Lithium-iron-phosphate 51 V 60 Ah 3,100 Wh // Type of drive: center motor 9,000 W 12 PS
Max. range: 45 mi / 70 km // Speed: 50 mph / 80 km/h // Design: Team eRockit

SHOWSTOPPER

PG // BLACKBLOCK 2

Stars like Lady Gaga and Orlando Bloom ride showpieces made by PG. Run by young entrepreneur Manuel Ostner, this Regensburg-based company is uncompromising in the use of high tech to satisfy its customers' individual desires. Either by means of an app, or on PG's website, customers can select from 60 million different options for customizing their individual bike. The one-of-a-kind frames are handcrafted and the customer-selected options are assembled by hand. One highlight: The 1,000 watt all-wheel drive with regeneration makes it particularly easy to cruise the streets on this speed pedelec model.

Stars wie Lady Gaga und Orlando Bloom fahren auf die Showstücke von PG ab. Die Regensburger Company um Jungunternehmer Manuel Ostner setzt kompromisslos Hightech um, so individuell, wie ihre Kunden es wünschen. In der App oder auf der Website kann man sich aus 60 Millionen Möglichkeiten sein individuelles Bike zusammenstellen. Die Rahmen der Unikate werden handgefertigt und auch die Kundenwünsche werden manuell montiert. Ein Highlight: der 1000-Watt-Allradantrieb mit Rekuperationsfunktion. Damit lässt es sich in der S-Pedelec-Variante besonders bequem über die Straßen cruisen.

Country: Germany // Year: 2012 // Weight: 88 lb / 40 kg // Frame: hand-welded steel frame
Gears: 8-speed Shimano XT with gripshift // Tires: 26" // Brakes: Magura MT2 hydraulic brakes
Battery: BMZ Lithium-Ion 36 V 13.5 Ah 486 Wh // Type of drive: All-wheel Heinzmann wheel hub motor 1,000 W
(speed pedelec version) // Max. range: 25 mi / 40 km // Speed: 28 mph / 45 km/h // Design: PG

TWO AS ONE

FLYER // TANDEM

There is something inherently romantic about tandems. Couples pulling together—or better yet, pedaling on the same chain. What is special about the Flyer Tandem is that the cranks are not synchronized and are actually disengaged while freewheeling. This means that one of the riders can take a break while the other takes over as the chauffeur, riding with electric assistance. The tandem is equipped with a push assist and a clever lighting system. In addition to a daytime light, a sensor automatically switches on additional lighting when it gets dark. This ensures that lovers can pedal off into the sunset together—and that they'll make it home safely after dark.

Tandems haben etwas Urromantisches an sich. Paare ziehen am selben Strang – oder besser: Sie treten in dieselbe Kette. Das Besondere am Flyer Tandem ist, dass die Kurbeln nicht synchronisiert und im Freilauf entkoppelt sind. Dadurch kann einer der Fahrer aussetzen und der andere chauffiert ihn mit Elektrounterstützung durch die Gegend. Das Tandem verfügt über einen Schiebemodus und eine clevere Lichtanlage. Neben Taglicht schaltet ein Sensor bei Dunkelheit automatisch Licht dazu. So können Verliebte gemeinsam in den Sonnenuntergang radeln und landen anschließend im Dunkeln wieder sicher zu Hause.

Country: Germany // Year: 2011 // Weight: 88 lb / 40 kg // Frame: aluminum
Gears: 10-speed Shimano XT chain drive // Tires: 26" // Brakes: Magura Louise hydraulic disc brakes
Battery: Panasonic Lithium-Ion 36 V 13.2 Ah 476 Wh // Type of drive: Panasonic center motor 250 W
Max. range: 30 mi / 50 km // Speed: 15 mph / 25 km/h // Design: Flyer and 360° Engineering

Country: Switzerland // Year: 2012 // Weight: 64 lb / 29 kg // Frame: aluminum // Gears: SRAM X-7 27-speed derailleur // Tires: 26"

Brakes: Avid Single Digit 7 V-brakes / Avid BB7 disc brakes // Battery: Lithium-Ion Manganese 36 V 20 Ah 720 Wh

Type of drive: Dolphin rear wheel hub motor 500 W // Max. range: 60 mi / 100 km // Speed: 25 mph / 40 km/h // Design: Michael Kutter

L.A. CONFIDENTIAL

DOLPHIN // EXPRESS

Dolphin's designer is Basel native Michael Kutter, who was already designing and building e-bike prototypes back in 1992 and was responsible for developing the principle of pedelecs. Since then he has been consistently working on implementing his futuristic mobility concepts. His bikes are known for their high performance, long range, and enormous power for handling hills. It comes as no surprise that the latest generation of Dolphins are also the most powerful e-bikes on the Swiss market. The Los Angeles Police Department has recognized that the Dolphin Express is an environmentally friendly alternative to cars and its police officers are now riding Dolphins on patrol.

Designer des Dolphin ist der Basler Michael Kutter, der bereits 1992 Prototypen von E-Bikes entworfen und gebaut und das Prinzip der Pedelecs entwickelt hat. Seither arbeitet er konsequent an der Umsetzung seiner Mobilitätskonzepte von morgen. Leistungsstärke, eine große Reichweite und eine enorme Zugkraft am Berg sind charakteristisch für seine Räder. So ist die neueste Generation des Dolphin denn auch das leistungsstärkste E-Bike auf dem Schweizer Markt. Inzwischen hat auch die Polizei von Los Angeles die umweltfreundliche Alternative zum Auto erkannt und fährt auf Dolphins Patrouille.

LOVING IT
KAREN GRAJEDA ON NYCEWHEELS // ELECTRIC BROMPTON

Country: United Kingdom
Year: 2010
Weight: 44 lb / 20 kg
Frame: butted chromoly steel
Gears: 3-speed Shimano internal gear shifter
Tires: 16"
Brakes: dual pivot caliper
Battery: Lithium Polymer 10 Ah or 15 Ah
Type of drive: brushless front wheel hub motor 250 W
Max. range: 20 mi / 32 km
Speed: 20 mph / 32 km/h
Design: Andrew Ritchey, Rupert Cebular

Shortly after completing her degree in economics, Karen Grajeda landed her dream job at the United Nations. She would be staying in Manhattan for at least five years! She settled down in Turtle Bay on the eastern edge of Midtown. Karen is proud of her adopted home—as are many New Yorkers. And like most people who live in Manhattan, Karen does not own her own car.

The young woman from Guatemala is environmentally conscious. At the same time, she was looking for a comfortable mode of transportation to navigate New York traffic. It didn't take long for her to decide on an e-bike.

"It is amazing how your perception of beauty changes when you're in love," says Karen. But she isn't referring to her husband. She has fallen head over heels for her new Brompton e-bike, and she's sure that this feeling will last forever.

‖‖

IN MOST RESTAURANTS AND CAFES, I CAN SIMPLY PUT IT UNDER THE TABLE.

‖‖

The Brompton is considered to be one of the best foldable e-bikes on the market. Although its frame is small, anyone can ride it comfortably. It is classic, British, and is precision-assembled by hand in the heart of London. In just four easy steps, you can fold the bicycle into a small, easy-to-manage package: Park the back wheel, fold the main frame, swing down the handlebar, and lower the saddle—done! The entire process takes barely 20 seconds. The ingenuity of the design speaks for itself. With its ability to quickly transform into a compact package, the Brompton is very easy to carry up the stairs, or take into a crammed elevator. What's even better, you can easily take it with you on buses, taxis, and subways, travel straight through the city and then, at the other end, simply bike back. "I love my folding bike," raves Karen. "I can take it everywhere. I don't have to lock it up outside and worry that it will have been stolen when I return. In most restaurants and cafés, I can simply put it under the table."

Karen does errands on her e-bike, uses it to transport groceries, and rides to spinning and yoga classes. "It's Manhattan. Of course you need to have a bit of courage, but I feel safe on the streets here," she says. New York ranks eighth among the most bicycle-friendly cities in the United States, and Mayor Michael Bloomberg is a huge proponent of making the city even more bicycle-friendly. Almost 500 miles of bike paths already wend their way through the Big Apple—and Karen is thankful for that fact every single day.

Kurz nachdem sie ihr Wirtschaftsstudium abgeschlossen hatte, ergatterte Karen Grajeda ihren Traumjob bei den Vereinten Nationen. Für mindestens fünf Jahre würde sie in Manhattan bleiben! Also richtete sie sich in Turtle Bay ein, im Osten von Midtown. Karen ist stolz auf ihre Wahlheimat – so wie viele New Yorker. Und so wie die meisten Manhattanites besitzt Karen kein eigenes Auto.

Die junge Frau aus Guatemala lebt umweltbewusst. Gleichzeitig suchte sie nach einem bequemen Transportmittel, um sich durch den New Yorker Verkehr zu schlängeln. Da lag die Entscheidung für ein E-Bike nahe.

„Es ist schon beeindruckend, wie sehr sich die Wahrnehmung von Schönheit ändert, wenn man verliebt ist", sagt Karen. Dabei bezieht sie sich aber nicht auf ihren Ehemann. Hals über Kopf hat sie sich in ihr neues E-Bike von Brompton verliebt und ist sich sicher, dass diese Liebe immer halten wird.

Das Brompton gilt als eines der besten klappbaren E-Bikes auf dem Markt. Auch wenn der Rahmen klein ist, kann jeder bequem darauf fahren. Es ist klassisch, britisch und wird im Herzen Londons in präziser Handarbeit zusammengebaut. Mit nur vier schnellen Griffen kriegt man das Rad handlich klein: Hinterrad einklappen, Mittelteil falten, Lenker umdrehen und Sitz runterschrauben – fertig! Das alles dauert nicht länger als 20 Sekunden. Die Genialität des Designs spricht für sich. Und die Fähigkeit des Brompton, schnell ein kompaktes Paket zu werden, spricht dafür, es einfach die Treppen hochzutragen. Oder mit in einen engen Aufzug zu nehmen. Noch besser ist natürlich, dass man damit ganz einfach in Busse, Taxen und U-Bahnen steigen, quer durch die Stadt fahren und am anderen Ende einfach wieder weiterradeln kann. „Ich liebe mein Klapprad", schwärmt Karen. „Ich kann es überallhin mitnehmen; ich muss es nicht draußen anschließen und Angst haben, dass es geklaut worden ist, wenn ich wiederkomme. In den meisten Restaurants und Cafés kann ich es einfach unter den Tisch stellen."

Karen fährt mit ihrem E-Bike, wenn sie Besorgungen macht, Lebensmittel nach Hause transportiert, und um zu ihren Spinning- und Yogakursen zu kommen. „It's Manhattan. Natürlich braucht man etwas Mut, aber ich fühle mich auf den Straßen hier sicher", sagt sie. New York ist auf Platz acht der fahrradfreundlichsten Städte in Amerika. Auch weil sich der amtierende Bürgermeister Bloomberg dafür starkmacht, die Stadt noch fahrradtauglicher zu gestalten. Schon jetzt verlaufen über 800 Kilometer Radwege durch den Big Apple. Eine Tatsache, über die sich Karen jeden Tag wieder freut.

UNCHAINED

MANDO FOOTLOOSE // MANDO FOOTLOOSE

With this model, pedaling transforms mechanical energy into electricity, which in turn charges the e-bike's battery. This in itself is nothing unusual, but this folding bike from South Korea functions without the typical chain seen on a bicycle. This means that riders don't need to worry about getting grease on their pant legs and are also spared that desperate attempt to get the chain back on the sprocket after changing a flat tire. A particularly practical feature: The Mando Footloose can be rolled even after it has been folded. This makes it possible for riders to quickly bring it into the house and use it as a stationary exercise bike.

Beim Treten verwandelt sich mechanische Energie in elektrische, die wiederum den Akku des E-Bikes speist. Das ist an sich nichts Ungewöhnliches, aber dieses Klapprad aus Südkorea funktioniert ohne fahrradtypische Kette. Somit bleiben Hosenbeine von Löchern und Schmieröl verschont und Fahrradfahrer vor Pannen und dem verzweifelten Versuch bewahrt, die Kette wieder auf das Zahnrad zu zerren. Besonders praktisch: Sogar zusammengeklappt ist das Mando Footloose immer noch rollbar. So kann es schnell ins Haus geschoben und dort als Hometrainer genutzt werden.

Country: South Korea // Year: 2013 // Weight: 48 lb / 21.7 kg // Frame: aluminum // Gears: 2 // Tires: 20" // Brakes: Mando disc brakes

Battery: Lithium-Ion 36 V 8.2 Ah 300 Wh // Type of drive: Mando Dual winding rear wheel hub motor 250 W // Max. range: 30 mi / 45 km

Speed: 15 mph / 25 km/h // Design: Mark Sanders

THE LIGHTEST E-BIKE ON EARTH

EEGO NOAHK I // E-MICRO-BIKE EEGOTWINDRIVE

Small but mighty! In less than five seconds, the handlebars and saddle can be collapsed into the compact size of a carry-on bag and this folding bike can be easily stowed in the trunk of a car or under an office desk. The biggest asset of the Noahk I TwinDrive has to be its weight: At just 20 pounds including battery, it is the lightest e-bike in the world—the ideal traveling companion for urban commuters or city residents on the move.

Klein, aber oho! In weniger als fünf Sekunden können Lenker und Sattel kompakt zusammengefaltet werden und das Klapprad lässt sich wie Handgepäck im Kofferraum oder unterm Bürotisch verstauen. Der größte Trumpf des Noahk I TwinDrive ist sicherlich das Gewicht: Mit seinen neun Kilogramm inklusive Akku ist es das leichteste E-Bike der Welt – der ideale Reisebegleiter für urbane Pendler oder agile Großstädter.

Country: Austria // Year: 2012 // Weight: 20 lb / 9 kg // Frame: magnesium // Gears: no gears

Tires: 16" // Brakes: eegoBeltBrake // Battery: Lithium-Ion 15 V 12 Ah 150 Wh

Type of drive: eegoThinCake front wheel hub motor 120 W // Max. range: 30 mi / 50 km

Speed: 12 mph / 20 km/h // Design: eego e-mobility GmbH

CATERPILLAR ON WHEELS

MOBIKY // YOURI 16

It takes just three seconds to collapse this innovative folding bike made by French manufacturer Mobiky-Tech, and it can still be rolled afterwards: Although the frame becomes small and compact, the wheels remain on the ground. That means it's easy for riders to take this little black number from France onto the bus or train and to bring it along on trips. The wheels measure just 16 inches, and they are given a helping hand by the Shimano gear shift with eight speeds and by the motor. So, there is nothing standing in the way of longer rides.

Dieses innovative Klapprad des französischen Herstellers Mobiky-Tech ist innerhalb von drei Sekunden zusammen-gefaltet und immer noch gut zu rollen: Der Rahmen wird klein, doch beide Räder bleiben auf dem Boden. So lässt sich das kleine Schwarze aus Frankreich bequem in Bus und Bahn mitnehmen und auf Reisen leicht verstauen. Die Räder messen gerade einmal 16 Zoll, wobei die Shimano-Gangschaltung mit acht Gängen und der Motor für einen guten Ausgleich sorgen. Längeren Fahrten steht also nichts im Weg.

Country: France // Year: 2011 // Weight: 42 lb / 19,2 kg // Frame: aluminum // Gears: 8-speed Shimano Nexus
Tires: 16" // Brakes: front: Shimano V-brakes, rear: Nexus roller brakes // Battery: Lithium-Ion 24 V 11 Ah 264 Wh
Type of drive: 250 W // Max. range: 35 mi / 60 km // Speed: 15 mph / 25 km/h // Design: Mobiky-Tech

Country: United Kingdom // Year: 2012 // Weight: 34 lb / 15,6 kg // Frame: injection-molded magnesium
Gears: 3-speed Shimano Nexus with electronic shifting // Tires: 20" // Brakes: hydraulic disc brakes
Battery: Lithium-Ion 22 V 10.75 Ah 236 Wh // Type of drive: Gocycle G2 front wheel hub motor 250 W
Max. range: 40 mi / 65 km // Speed: 20 mph / 32 km/h // Design: Karbon Kinetics Ltd

THE FORMULA 1 BIKE

GOCYCLE // GOCYCLE G2R

When a renowned British automotive engineer designs his own bicycle, the result is a futuristic vehicle perfect for city centers worldwide. A clean-running micro-motor drive, fully enclosed Cleandrive, and electronic 3-speed gear shift are just as important to Richard Thorpe, who used to work for McLaren, as a compact design for convenient transport and space-efficient storage. The frame and the removable PitstopWheels are made of light-weight injection-molded magnesium, a first for this category.

Entwirft ein englischer Nobelauto-Ingenieur ein eigenes Rad, entsteht ein futuristisches Mobil, perfekt für die Innenstadt der Metropolen dieses Planeten. Sauberer Antrieb durch Mikromotor, gekapselter Cleandrive und elektronische Shimano 3-Gang-Schaltung waren Richard Thorpe, der für McLaren arbeitete, genauso wichtig wie ein kompaktes Design für den angenehmen Transport und die platzsparende Aufbewahrung. Rahmen und schnell demontierbare PitstopWheels bestehen aus leichtem, gegossenem Magnesium, ein Novum für diese Kategorie.

MULTIFUNCTIONAL

VOLTITUDE SA // VOLTITUDE V1

It looks like a Swiss Army knife and is every bit as practical and universal in its function. The Voltitude combines an original design with everyday usability and minimal storage dimensions. When folded, this snazzy Swiss folding bike is only 24 inches wide and 33 inches tall. The low center of gravity, disc brakes, and normal wheelbase carry this red speedster—made of recycled aluminum—quickly and safely through the maze of city traffic.

Sieht aus wie ein Schweizer Taschenmesser, funktioniert auch so praktisch und universell. Das Voltitude kombiniert originelles Design mit Alltagstauglichkeit und minimalen Staumaßen. Das pfiffige Schweizer Klapprad weist zusammengelegt in Breite und Höhe nur 60 auf 85 Zentimeter auf. Im Stadtverkehr bringen der tiefe Schwerpunkt, die Scheibenbremsen und der normale Radstand den roten Flitzer aus recyceltem Aluminium schnell und sicher durchs Verkehrsgetümmel.

Country: Switzerland // Year: 2012 // Weight: 59.5 lb / 27 kg // Frame: CNC aluminum // Gears: 7-speed Shimano Nexus

Tires: 12" // Brakes: Shimano hydraulic disc brakes // Battery: Panasonic Lithium-Ion 36 V 11.6 Ah 418 Wh

Type of drive: Daum Electronic center motor 250 W // Max. range: 25 mi / 40 km // Speed: 15 mph / 25 km/h

Design: André-Marcel Collombin, Cyrille Gay

孙乃逊

MR. SUN ON SHANGHAI KAISHUN DOUBLE-SHOULDER LOADER KING

Country: China
Tires: 22"

孙乃逊

Sun Naixun 孙乃逊 has operated a flower and plant business in Shanghai for decades. His store is located on Shaanxi Nan Lu, a busy shopping street in Huang Pu, one of Shanghai's eight older districts in its center. Sycamore trees line the streets of old Shanghai—a beautiful legacy from the French who established their concession in this district in the second half of the 19th century, reshaping the area to reflect European taste. Naixun has been riding an e-bike for years. Electric bicycles are everywhere in China; they have replaced traditional bicycles as the country's primary means of transportation. While in Europe e-bikes are a luxury product, in China they are a standard form of private transportation. Millions of Chinese use them: Over 22 million e-bikes were sold in 2012 alone. Gasoline and vehicles with internal combustion engines are expensive yet coveted, so many who use e-bikes are saving money so they can get a bit closer to the dream of owning their own car.

Clusters of cyclists riding e-bikes form at every red light, and many cyclists wear a face mask and plastic arm and leg coverings to protect themselves from the dirt and smog of this huge metropolis. As soon as the light turns green, they take off, e-bikes humming, and scatter into the chaotic traffic. Naixun uses his e-bike to deliver flowers and plants to customers and to pick up goods from the market. "It's comfortable and inexpensive," explains the 38-year-old. After work, he also uses his e-bike to drive home to an outlying district of Shanghai. He would be completely lost without his e-bike. It was terrible when it was stolen in 2008: "I was incredibly sad—and angry at the thief."

I'D REALLY LIKE TO BUY A CAR.

Naixun did not have a choice—he had to buy himself a new e-bike. "Unfortunately, the batteries in my new one aren't as powerful. They wear out quickly and I have to replace them every year." Since the old flower market moved four years ago, Naixun's business isn't as good as it was in the past. "I'm thinking about moving back to my hometown in Jiangsu province. But I'd like to earn more money first, because I'd really like to buy a car."

Sun Naixun 孙乃逊 betreibt seit Jahrzehnten ein Blumen- und Pflanzengeschäft in Schanghai. Sein Laden liegt auf der Shaanxi Nan Lu, einer belebten Einkaufsstraße in Huang Pu, einem der acht alten „inneren" Bezirke Schanghais. Hier, im alten Schanghai, säumen Platanen die Straßen – ein hübsches Erbe der Franzosen, die in diesem Viertel in der zweiten Hälfte des 19. Jahrhunderts ihre Konzession gründeten und den Bezirk nach europäischem Geschmack umformten. Es ist viele Jahre her, dass Naixun zum ersten Mal auf einem E-Bike saß. In China sieht man Elektro-Fahrräder überall, sie haben das traditionelle Rad als Fortbewegungsmittel der Nation ersetzt. Anders als in Europa sind E-Bikes hier kein Luxusprodukt, sondern Standard im Individualverkehr. Millionen Chinesen nutzen sie: Allein 2012 wurden über 22 Millionen Stück verkauft. Benzin und Fahrzeuge mit Verbrennungsmotor sind teuer und so kommen viele mit einem E-Bike dem Traum vom eigenen Auto ein wenig näher.

An jeder roten Ampel bilden sich Schwärme von E-Bikefahrern, viele mit Mundschutz und Plastiküberziehern an Armen und Beinen, um sich vor dem Schmutz und Smog der Megametropole zu schützen. Summend düsen sie los, sobald die Ampel auf Grün umspringt, und verstreuen sich im chaotischen Verkehr. Naixun fährt mit seinem E-Bike Blumen und Pflanzen zu den Kunden und holt Ware aus dem Großmarkt. „Es ist bequem und kostet nicht viel", erklärt der 38-Jährige. Er braucht sein E-Bike auch, um von seinem Geschäft nach Hause zu fahren, in einen Randbezirk von Schanghai. Ohne das Fahrzeug ist er aufgeschmissen. Umso schlimmer, als sein Rad 2008 gestohlen wurde: „Ich war unfassbar traurig und wütend auf den Dieb."

Naixun hatte keine Wahl und musste sich ein neues E-Bike kaufen. „Leider sind bei meinem jetzigen Modell die Batterien nicht so leistungsstark. Sie nutzen sich schnell ab und ich muss jedes Jahr den Akku austauschen." Seit der alte Blumenmarkt vor vier Jahren umgezogen ist, läuft Naixuns Geschäft nicht mehr so gut wie früher. „Ich denke darüber nach, in meine Heimatstadt in der Provinz Jiangsu zurückzukehren. Aber vorher will ich noch mehr Geld verdienen – ich würde mir gerne ein Auto kaufen."

JUICED UP!

JUICED RIDERS // ODK U500 E-BIKE

During his competition years, former U.S. high jump Olympian Tora Harris noticed the constant rise of e-bikes in China. Afterwards he decided to stay and learn how to build e-bikes for himself. Today, the founder of Juiced Riders produces the small and agile ODK U500 cargo bike. Of special note is the 48-volt battery; rated at 720 watt-hours, it is one of the most powerful on the market. This e-bike can be tailored to meet a wide range of needs using accessories such as child seats, baskets, boxes, and panniers.

Schon während seiner Zeit als Hochsprung-Olympionike erlebte der US-Amerikaner Tora Harris den stetigen Aufstieg des E-Bikes in China. Anschließend blieb er, um das Selberbauen von E-Bikes zu erlernen. Heute produziert der Gründer von Juiced Riders das kleine, wendige Lastenrad ODK U500. Ein besonderes Augenmerk liegt auf den 48-Volt-Akkus, die mit 720 Wattstunden zu den stärksten am Markt zählen. Durch zahlreiche Accessoires wie Kindersitze, Körbe, Boxen und Radtaschen wird das E-Bike den unterschiedlichsten Bedürfnissen gerecht.

Country: China // Year: 2012 // Weight: 72.5 lb / 32.9 kg // Frame: 6061 aluminum // Gears: 3–7 speed Shimano Internal // Tires: 20"

Brakes: Promax DSK 715 disc brakes // Battery: Lithium-Ion 48 V 15 Ah 720 Wh // Type of drive: 8FUN BPM front wheel hub motor 500 W

Max. range: 50 mi / 80 km // Speed: 20 mph / 32 km/h // Design: Tora Harris

SHOPPING AROUND

KTM FAHRRAD GMBH // KTM ESHOPPER

As indicated in its name, the eShopper was designed for shopping trips and hopes to encourage riders to leave their cars at home when they run short errands. The bike's robust frame is an award-winning special design that ensures that the cargo baskets won't sag under the weight of shopping. The hydraulic brakes ensure that the eShopper will come to a safe stop even when fully loaded. The maximum permitted weight is a hefty 330 pounds. In 2012, the eShopper was the only e-bike to win gold in the Eurobike Design Award.

Wie sich am Namen eShopper zeigt, wurde dieses Bike für private Einkaufstouren entwickelt und soll Nutzer dazu bewegen, das Auto für ihre kurzen Einkaufswege stehen zu lassen. Der verstärkte Rahmen des Bikes ist eine preisgekrönte Spezialentwicklung und verhindert, dass sich der Gepäckträger unter den Neuanschaffungen durchbiegt. Die hydraulischen Bremsen sorgen dafür, dass der eShopper auch im Falle einer Maximalbeladung rechtzeitig zum Stehen kommt. Stolze 150 Kilogramm sind das höchstzulässige Gesamtgewicht. Als einziges E-Bike erhielt er 2012 den Eurobike Design Award in Gold.

Country: Austria // Year: 2011 // Weight: 59 lb / 26.9 kg // Frame: aluminum

Gears: 8-speed Shimano Alfine Rapidfire // Tires: 24" // Brakes: Shimano Deore hydraulic disc brakes

Battery: Bosch Lithium-Ion 36 V 8 Ah 288 Wh // Type of drive: Bosch center motor 250 W

Max. range: 60 mi / 100 km // Speed: 15 mph / 25 km/h // Design: KTM Fahrrad GmbH

VINTAGE ITALIAN

EL CICLO // MUGNAIA

Be it beer crates, boxes, or children—you can load almost anything that isn't nailed down onto the El ciclo Mugnaia. This Italian bike has a front cargo platform that can carry 33 pounds and a long rear rack that can handle a load of 110 pounds. Two storage areas next to the rear tires make it easy to securely fasten cargo. Hats off to anyone who takes full advantage of the cargo space to load this e-bike up with both a child seat and the weekly groceries at the same time!

Ob mit Bierkisten, Kartons oder Kindern – das El ciclo Mugnaia kann mit fast allem beladen werden, was nicht niet- und nagelfest ist. Das italienische Rad hat eine Frontabstellfläche für 15 Kilogramm und einen auffällig langen Gepäckträger mit einer Traglast von 50 Kilogramm. Zwei Ablageflächen neben dem Hinterreifen erleichtern die stabile Befestigung. Respekt vor dem, der die Vollbeladung mit Kindersitz und Wocheneinkauf ausnutzt!

Country: Italy // Year: 2011 // Weight: 57 lb / 26 kg // Frame: aluminum alloy

Gears: 7-speed Shimano Alivio 13/34T // Tires: front 20", rear 26"

Brakes: front: mechanical disc brake 160 mm, rear: V-brake by Saccon

Battery: Lithium LiFePO4 36 V 12 Ah 432 Wh // Type of drive: 8Fun SWXH rear wheel hub motor 250 W

Max. range: 50 mi / 80 km // Speed: 15 mph / 25 km/h // Design: El ciclo

BEAUTY QUEEN

RIESE & MÜLLER // LOAD HYBRID LIGHT

With its low-slung cargo area, the Load hybrid makes it easy to stow even heavy loads with little effort. The cargo area can accommodate two beer crates side by side, or a child seat. Thanks to the full suspension, riders don't need to worry about the weight of either glass bottles or children. The maximum permitted weight is 440 pounds. The adaptability of the Load hybrid is astounding, because when necessary the bicycle can even be taken apart for storage. In 2013 the bicycle received the iF product design award.

Das Load hybrid erlaubt es, mit seiner tief positionierten Transportfläche auch schwere Lasten mit wenig Kraftanstrengung einzuladen. Genau zwei Bierkisten passen nebeneinander hinein, optional auch ein Kindersitz. Um Glasflaschen und Nachwuchs muss man sich dank Vollfederung aber keine Sorgen machen. Das zulässige Gesamtgewicht beträgt 200 Kilogramm. Erstaunlich sind auch die Verwandlungskünste des Load hybrid, denn das Rad lässt sich bei Bedarf auseinandernehmen und verstauen. Das Bike hat 2013 den iF product design award gewonnen.

Country: Germany // Year: 2012 // Weight: 66 lb / 30 kg // Frame: aluminum 7005 T6 TIG-welded
Gears: 9-speed Shimano Deore // Tires: front 20", rear 26" // Brakes: Tektro Auriga SUB disc brakes
Battery: Bosch Lithium-Ion 36 V 8.2 Ah 300 Wh or 11 Ah 400 Wh // Type of drive: Bosch center motor 250 W
Max. range: 120 mi / 190 km // Speed: 15 mph / 25 km/h // Design: Stijn Deferm

ONE FOR ALL

RADKUTSCHE // MUSKETIER

A successful blend of pleasant cargo transport and environmentally friendly mobility: Whether used for a large family shopping trip or to deliver goods, the maneuverable Musketier quietly transports its load from point A to point B. Yet it is not above being used for more creative applications. The cargo platform (47 x 32 inches) is large enough to accommodate a mobile crêperie or to install a mobile sound system. And this powerful tricycle is a helpful companion even for days that don't involve crêpes and music: It can handle loads of up to 660 pounds.

Eine gelungene Mischung aus angenehmem Lastentransport und umweltfreundlicher Fortbewegung: Sei es der große Familieneinkauf oder eine Warenlieferung, das Musketier bringt wendig und leise die Ladung von A nach B. Auch für eine kreative Umnutzung ist es sich nicht zu schade. Auf der Ladefläche (120 mal 80 Zentimeter) kann man zum Beispiel eine fahrbare Crêperie aufbauen oder eine mobile Soundanlage installieren. Und auch an Tagen ohne Crêpes und Musik ist das starke Dreirad ein hilfreicher Begleiter: Mit bis zu 300 Kilogramm kann es beladen werden.

Country: Germany // Year: 2012 // Weight: 132 lb / 60 kg // Frame: steel // Gears: Nuvinci // Tires: 24"
Brakes: Tektro hydraulic disc brakes // Battery: Samsung Lithium-Ion 37 V 56 Ah 2,072 Wh
Type of drive: eZeebike front wheel hub motor 500 W // Max. range: 60 mi / 100 km
Speed: 15 mph / 25 km/h // Design: Stefan Rickmeyer

THE GREEN MESSENGER
URBAN-E // IBULLITT

The Urban-e can transport a packing box weighing up to 220 pounds. That's why this model is a favorite of small urban businesses and courier services. On sunny days, the optional solar panel charges the battery even while you're riding it. This cargo bike has a comparatively narrow design to ensure that riders can elegantly weave their way between cars in city traffic.

Eine Umzugskiste mit einer Last von 100 Kilogramm kann das Urban-e transportieren. Besonders beliebt ist diese Variante daher im städtischen Kleingewerbe und im Kurierdienst. Das optionale Solarpanel lädt den Akku an Sonnentagen schon während der Fahrt wieder auf. Das Transport-Bike ist vergleichsweise schlank konzipiert, damit der Fahrer sich im Stadtverkehr elegant zwischen Autos hindurchschlängeln kann.

Country: Germany // Year: 2011 // Weight: 88 lb / 40 kg // Frame: aluminum // Gears: 8-speed Shimano Alfine hub gears

Tires: front 20", rear 26" // Brakes: Shimano Alfine hydraulic disc brakes // Battery: Samsung Lithium-Ion 36 V 14–44 Ah max. 1,584 Wh

Type of drive: Urban-e front wheel hub motor 250 W // Max. range: 155 mi / 250 km // Speed: 15 mph / 25 km/h

Design: Larry vs Harry (frame), Urban-e Design (box / electric)

"E"-MAIL

MIRKO WASIC ON MIFA // E-BIKE III

Country: Germany
Year: 2011
Weight: 128 lb / 58 kg
Gears: 5-speed hub gear
Tires: 26"
Brakes: parking brake and service brake
Battery: lithium iron phosphate
Max. range: 12 mi / 20 km
Design: Mitteldeutsche Fahrradwerke AG

Deutsche Post

Mirko Wasic is 41 years old and has been working as a letter carrier for the Deutsche Post for twenty years. His employer provided him with an e-bike for health and safety reasons because his delivery area has many hills. "It is so much nicer! I don't have to pedal as hard any more— the batteries now do the heavy work for me," remarks the Berlin native. The use of e-bikes relieves letter carriers of the physically strenuous work, especially starting off with a full load. And the reality is that letter carriers are stopping and starting all day long, making their way from one house to the next. Approximately 6,100 letter carriers from the Deutsche Post now ride e-bikes on their delivery routes. Another 17,300 traditional bicycles are powered by muscle strength alone.

I DON'T HAVE TO PEDAL AS HARD ANY MORE— THE BATTERIES NOW DO THE HEAVY WORK FOR ME.

In 1999, the Deutsche Post began experimenting with various e-bike models. E-bikes have been used for mail delivery in the German postal service since 2001. The first e-bikes were developed in collaboration with Biria and Kynast.

Mirko rides the latest model featuring a front hub motor that is available through the postal service's vehicle fleet: an e-bike with a battery box and Heinzmann technology made by Deutsche Post partner Mittel- deutsche Fahrradwerke AG (MIFA). This is already the third generation of bicycles with electrical assistance used by the postal service, but Mirko has only been riding an e-bike for about six months.

Needless to say, the first day Mirko set out on his delivery route on his new vehicle was an unusual one. "I noticed that it wasn't as hard to pedal. I just twisted the handle and it took right off," he explains.

The bicycles at Deutsche Post were replaced in stages. The inventory of e-bikes is currently being updated. New third generation e-bikes are replacing 1,800 of the first generation ones.

Mirko starts work every morning at 6:30 a.m., loading his delivery bike, heading off into the city at about 9:30 a.m. Mirko estimates that every day he spends about six hours covering his ten-mile route.

"I am so happy that I now have the e-bike. It also has a setting that is really helpful when there's snow on the ground and it's hard to ride. In that mode, the batteries propel the e-bike along by itself at a little over 3 mph, and I can walk comfortably next to it." Once he's done with his route and has delivered all the mail, Mirko returns the e-bike to his delivery base. There it is charged overnight so it is ready for use first thing the next morning.

Mirko Wasic ist 41 Jahre alt und arbeitet seit 20 Jahren als Briefträger für die Deutsche Post. Das E-Bike stellte ihm sein Arbeitgeber zur Verfügung – aus gesundheits- und arbeitsschutztechnischen Gründen in Zustellbezirken mit vielen Steigungen. „Das ist viel angenehmer! Ich muss einfach nicht mehr so viel strampeln, das machen jetzt die Akkus für mich", sagt der Berliner. Der Einsatz von E-Bikes erleichtert die körperlich anstrengende Arbeit der Postboten, vor allem das Anfahren mit dem voll beladenen Rad. Und Postboten fahren im Grunde genommen den ganzen Tag an, vor jedem Haus aufs Neue. Inzwischen sind circa 6.100 Briefzusteller der Deutschen Post mit E-Bikes unterwegs. 17.300 Fahrräder werden von den Kollegen noch mit reiner Muskel- kraft gefahren.

1999 startete die Deutsche Post erste Betriebsversuche mit E-Bike- Modellen. Seit 2001 sind im Unternehmen bundesweit im Bereich der Briefzustellung E-Bikes im Einsatz. Die ersten wurden mit den Firmen Biria und Kynast entwickelt.

Mirko fährt das neueste Modell mit Frontnabenmotor, das im Fuhrpark der Post zur Verfügung steht: ein E-Bike mit Akku-Box und Heinzmann- Technik von der Firma MIFA Mitteldeutsche Fahrradwerke AG, mit der die Post heute zusammenarbeitet. Es ist schon die dritte Generation an Rädern mit elektrischer Unterstützung bei der Post, aber Mirko fährt erst seit einem guten halben Jahr mit einem E-Bike.

Natürlich war der erste Tag, an dem Mirko mit dem neuen Gefährt Briefe verteilte, ungewohnt. „Der Widerstand beim Strampeln ist nicht mehr so groß. Ich dreh' am Handgriff und das Ding fährt schnell an", erklärt er.

Die Fahrräder wurden in Etappen ausgetauscht. Aktuell erfolgt eine Verjüngung des E-Bike-Bestandes. 1 800 E-Bikes der ersten Generation werden durch neue Räder der dritten Generation ersetzt.

Jeden Morgen um 6.30 Uhr ist Dienstbeginn für Mirko. Dann belädt er sein Zustellrad und gegen 9.30 Uhr geht's raus in die Stadt. Mirko schätzt, dass er jeden Tag etwa 15 Kilometer zurücklegt. Dafür ist er ungefähr sechs Stunden unterwegs.

„Ich bin froh, dass ich das Teil jetzt hab'. Da ist auch 'n Schiebemodus dran, das wird im Winter wichtig, wenn in Berlin Schnee liegt und man nicht mehr gut fahren kann. Dann fährt das E-Bike von allein, so sechs Stundenkilometer, da kann ich bequem nebenherlaufen." Wenn er seine Tour abgefahren hat und alle Briefe ausgetragen sind, bringt Mirko das E-Bike zurück in seinen Zustellstützpunkt. Hier wird es über Nacht aufgeladen, damit es ihn am nächsten Tag mit neuer Kraft unterstützen kann.

KIDS AHOY

NIHOLA // NIHOLA FAMILY

Made in family-friendly Denmark, the Nihola Family is the best three-wheeled cargo bike for transporting children. Special steel tubing and seat belts offer protection in case of an accident. Colorful rain canopies for the cargo box keep the little ones dry if it happens to rain. Nihola is a company dedicated to special transportation needs: It offers models designed to accommodate wheelchairs, dogs, and advertising displays.

Das Nihola Family ist das beste dreirädrige Lastenfahrrad für Kindertransporte, das das familienfreundliche Dänemark zu bieten hat. Spezielle Stahlröhren und Gurte sorgen für Schutz im Falle eines Unfalls. Und damit die Kleinen im Trocknen bleiben, gibt es farbenfrohe Regenverdecke für den Transportkasten. Spezialtransporte liegen der Firma Nihola: Sie bietet auch Modelle zur Mitnahme von Rollstühlen, Hunden und Werbeaufstellern an.

Country: Denmark // Year: 2000 // Weight: 88 lb / 40 kg // Frame: steel // Gears: 8-speed Shimano Nexus 8
Tires: front 20", rear 26" // Brakes: front: Nihola drum brakes, rear: Nihola V-brakes
Battery: BionX Lithium-Ion 48 V 8.8 Ah 423 Wh // Type of drive: BionX rear wheel hub motor 200 W (AU & UK),
250 W (EU), 350 W (NA) // Max. range: 65 mi / 105 km // Speed: 15 mph / 25 km/h // Design: Niels Holme Larsen

FOR OCTOMUMS

VAN RAAM // GOCAB

|||||||||||||||||||||||||||||||||||||||||||||||||

Childcare workers know just how difficult it can be to keep track of eight young kids. The GoCab is designed specifically for daycare centers. Thanks to a cover, it can be used for excursions even in rainy weather. The small turning radius and a reverse gear make it easy to transport the whole gang. In 2011 Dutch bicycle manufacturer Van Raam won the prestigious Eurobike Award for this cargo electric bike.

Wer in der Kinderbetreuung arbeitet, weiß, wie schwierig es sein kann, acht kleine Racker zusammenzuhalten. Das GoCab ist speziell für Kindergärten konzipiert. Dank eines Verdecks können auch bei Regenwetter problemlos Ausflüge unternommen werden. Der kleine Wendekreis und ein Rückwärtsgang erleichtern das Befördern der Rasselbande. 2011 gewann der niederländische Radhersteller Van Raam mit diesem Lasten-Pedelec den renommierten Eurobike Award.

Country: Netherlands // Year: 2011 // Weight: 265.5 lb / 120 kg // Frame: steel // Gears: 8-speed Shimano
Tires: 20" // Brakes: Kailing hydraulic disc brakes // Battery: BMZ Lithium-Ion cobalt 36 V 25 Ah 900 Wh
Type of drive: Cristalite chain drive rear wheel axle 250 W // Max. range: 18 mi / 30 km // Speed: 9 mph / 15 km/h
Design: Van Der Veer Design

GROWN-UP TRIKE

PFAU-TEC // COMFORT

At first glance, this tricycle may seem reminiscent of bygone childhood days, yet it is a far cry from what you rode on as a toddler—the Comfort features a differential transmission and a front wheel hub motor that can achieve speeds of 12 miles per hour. This tricycle makes it possible for individuals who have difficulties with their coordination and/or balance to ride a bicycle. Pfau-Tec, a manufacturer based in Quakenbrück, has dedicated itself to the production of therapeutic bicycles and meets the high requirements of the German Medical Devices Directive. In addition, this model is a suitable option for overweight individuals.

Dieses Dreirad erinnert auf den ersten Blick an das Lieblingsgefährt aus Kindertagen. Doch weit gefehlt, denn das Comfort wartet mit Differentialgetriebe und einem 20 Stundenkilometer schnellen Frontmotor auf. Menschen, die koordinative und/oder Gleichgewichtsstörungen haben, wird damit das Fahrradfahren ermöglicht. Der Quakenbrücker Hersteller Pfau-Tec hat sich übrigens ganz der Herstellung von therapeutischen Fahrrädern verschrieben und erfüllt die hohen Anforderungen des Medizinproduktegesetzes. Auch für Übergewichtige ist diese Bike-Variante eine geeignete Radfahroption.

Country: Germany // Year: 2012 // Weight: 70.5 lb / 32 kg // Frame: steel tubing

Gears: 7-speed SRAM gearshift i-motion // Tires: 24"

Brakes: Shimano dual spring front-V-brake / coaster brakes

Battery: Ansmann or Heinzmann Lithium-Ion 36 V 9.0 Ah 250 Wh

Type of drive: Ansmann or Heinzmann front wheel hub motor 250 W

Max. range: 25 mi / 40 km // Speed: 12 mph / 20 km/h // Design: Pfau-Tec

FAMILY FUN

PACIFIC // 2RIDER ELECTRIC

This bike is designed for two riders but can optionally accommodate up to two additional child seats, offering riding pleasure for the entire family. The only downside is that children might not feel that they should have to ride their own bikes if their parents can drive them around so comfortably! Unlike conventional tandems, with this model there is no danger of tipping over when starting off or when braking at the same time. The 2Rider Electric is equipped with a torque sensor which measures the force applied while pedaling, and activates the motor as needed. This feature is particularly nice when you're biking uphill and loaded up with shopping and kids.

Dieses Rad ist für zwei Personen konzipiert, kann aber auch um zwei Kindersitze erweitert werden und bietet somit Fahrspaß für die ganze Familie. Nachteil: Kinder werden nicht mehr einsehen, warum sie selbst Rad fahren sollten, wenn Mama und Papa sie doch bequem kutschieren können. Anders als bei herkömmlichen Tandems besteht beim gemeinsamen Anfahren und Abbremsen nicht die Gefahr umzukippen. Das 2Rider Electric ist mit einem Drehmomentsensor ausgestattet, der die Trittkraft misst und je nach Bedarf den Motor einschaltet – besonders angenehm, wenn es bergauf geht und zu den Kids noch Einkäufe hinzukommen.

Country: Taiwan // Year: 2007 // Weight: 99 lb / 45 kg // Frame: aluminum 7005
Gears: 8-speed Shimano Alivio (12-34T) // Tires: 20" // Brakes: Tektro V-brakes 836AL
Battery: Porta Power Lithium-Ion 24 V 9 Ah 216 Wh // Type of drive: Sunstar center motor 250 W
Max. range: 35 mi / 60 km // Speed: 18 mph / 30 km/h // Design: George Lin

THAT EXTRA WHEEL

SCHACHNER GMBH // E-VIERRAD

The E-Vierrad from Austrian e-bike manufacturer Schachner offers an extra wheel. Stability and comfort were decisive features in the design. A low step-through and a saddle with a backrest make this e-bike particularly appealing to older individuals. The large basket on the rear of the bike makes it easy to transport purchases, and with just a little imagination the wide handlebars might give you the feeling you're riding a Harley Davidson.

Mit einem Rad mehr kann das E-Vierrad des österreichischen E-Bike-Herstellers Schachner aufwarten. Stabilität und Bequemlichkeit waren beim Bau maßgeblich. Ein tiefer Einstieg und ein Sattel mit Rückenlehne machen dieses E-Bike vor allem für ältere Menschen interessant. In dem großen Korb an der Rückseite kann man Einkäufe nach Hause befördern und mit etwas Fantasie lässt der breite Lenker dazu ein Harley-Davidson-Feeling aufkommen.

Country: Austria // Year: 2012 // Weight: 88 lb / 40 kg // Frame: aluminum // Gears: 3-speed Shimano internal gear shifter
Tires: front 20", rear 24" // Brakes: Artek disc brakes // Battery: Schachner Lithium-iron-phosphate (LiFePo4) 36 V 9 Ah 300 Wh
Type of drive: Schachner MM13 center motor 250 W // Max. range: 50 mi / 80 km // Speed: 15 mph / 25 km/h // Design: Franz Schachner

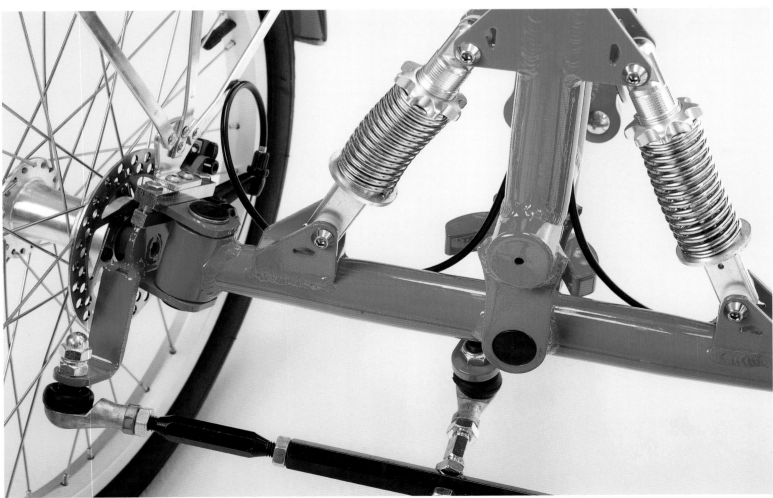

DESIGNER

NORBERT HALLER ON
A2B // HYBRID 24

Country: Germany

Year: 2011

Weight: 59 tb / 26.8 kg

Frame: heat-treated aluminum frame, powder-coated

Gears: 8-speed SRAM

Tires: 24"

Brakes: Magura MT4 hydraulic disc brakes

Battery: Sanyo Lithium-Ion 36 V 10 Ah 360 Wh

Type of drive: rear wheel hub motor 250 W

Max. range: 43.5 mi / 70 km

Speed: 15 mph / 25 km/h

Design: Norbert Haller, Hendrik Markowski, Michael Walinda, Alexander Brincker

Norbert Haller was already involved with e-bikes when he was working on his degree. While studying industrial design at the Berlin University of the Arts, he majored in vehicle design. "Initially I was more focused on bicycles, but then I designed an e-bike prototype for my thesis." That was back in 1998. "My colleagues and I often wondered why e-bikes were so incredibly ugly. They were plastic boxes on wheels— mobile vacuum cleaners with a steel structure and plastic cladding. The design was truly embarrassing." Laughing at himself, he adds: "We thought that we were such great designers and that we would change the world."

MY COLLEAGUES AND I OFTEN WONDERED WHY E-BIKES WERE SO INCREDIBLY UGLY.

Norbert explains that a different philosophy characterized the second generation of e-bikes. This time around the aim was to make the "e" in e-bike invisible. Everything having to do with the electric drive was reduced in size or hidden completely. In the meantime, some models have developed their own style. "You can see that it isn't a bicycle, that it's something new and different. Electromobility is beginning to develop its own stylistic language," says Norbert. And that was precisely his concept when he went into business with a colleague and designed the A2B bikes. "The trick is to strike the right balance between cost, production, design, and function. We have specialized in doing just that." Norbert discovered that it takes a while before you find meaningful compromises. "It goes without saying that you can use the best materials to develop the most extreme designs, but then you can't put them into serial production."

A2B is more than just one bike; it is an entire family ranging from e-bikes to e-scooters, available in different motor sizes. "The e-bike boom started about four years ago, and our A2B bikes influenced the market. I don't want to toot our own horn, but we were a player." Sales figures show that the image of e-bikes has changed. The automobile industry and government policies are pushing electromobility. Young people perceive e-bikes differently than they did a few years ago. An e-bike is a symbol of commitment to green mobility and no longer a sign of age and weakness. The willingness to spend $3,000 to $5,000 for an e-bike has grown.

"You have to work on highlighting the benefits and making the product attractive. That is what the e-bike industry has accomplished, and I think that our products played a part," says Norbert with more than a hint of pride. One example is the new frame design. Norbert consciously chose to avoid the classic bicycle frame and selected a powerful aluminum one as the foundation. The motor and batteries are so well integrated that the result is unique. "An honest design concept is important to me, something that is truly tailored to a new drive. The new drive needs an attractive design and shouldn't look like a vacuum cleaner."

Schon für sein Diplom hat sich Norbert Haller mit E-Bikes beschäftigt. Er studierte an der Universität der Künste in Berlin Industriedesign und legte während des Studiums einen Schwerpunkt auf Fahrzeugdesign. „Am Anfang waren es mehr Fahrräder, aber für die Diplomarbeit habe ich einen E-Bike-Prototyp designt." Das war 1998. „Meine Kollegen und ich haben uns damals oft gefragt, warum E-Bikes so unglaublich hässlich aussehen. Das waren fahrende Plastikboxen, fahrende Staubsauger aus einer Stahlkonstruktion mit 'ner Plastikverkleidung. Das Design war wirklich peinlich." Mit viel Selbstironie fügt er hinzu: „Da dachten wir uns, wir sind geile Designer und verändern jetzt die Welt."

Norbert erklärt, dass bei der zweiten Generation von E-Bikes ein anderer Gedanke prägend gewesen sei. Das „E" von E-Bike sollte unsichtbar bleiben. Alles, was auf den elektrischen Antrieb hinwies, wurde klein gemacht oder ganz versteckt. Inzwischen haben manche Modelle ihre eigene Stilsprache gefunden. „Man erkennt, das ist kein Fahrrad, das ist etwas Neues, etwas Eigenständiges. Die Elektromobilität beginnt ihre eigene Formsprache zu entwickeln", sagt Norbert. Genau das war auch sein Konzept, als er sich zusammen mit einem Kollegen selbstständig machte und die A2B-Bikes entwarf. „Die große Kunst ist es, die richtigen Kompromisse einzugehen zwischen Kosten, Produktion, Design und Funktion; darauf haben wir uns spezialisiert." Norbert hat die Erfahrung gemacht, dass es eine Weile dauert, bis man sinnvolle Mittelwege findet. „Natürlich kannst du die krassesten Designs mit den besten Materialien entwickeln, aber dann kannst du sie nicht in Serie produzieren."

A2B ist mehr als nur ein Bike, es ist eine ganze Familie: vom Pedelec bis zum E-Scooter, mit verschiedenen Motorleistungen. „Der E-Bike-Boom hat vor ungefähr vier Jahren angefangen und unsere A2B-Bikes haben den Markt beeinflusst. Ich will mich jetzt nicht über den grünen Klee loben, aber wir waren gut dabei." Die Verkaufszahlen zeigen, dass sich das Image des E-Bikes verändert hat. Elektromobilität wird inzwischen von der Autoindustrie und der Politik propagiert. Elektro-Räder werden von jungen Menschen heute anders aufgenommen als vor einigen Jahren. Mit einem E-Bike bekennt man sich zur Green Mobility, es gilt nicht mehr als Zeichen für Alter und Schwäche. Auch die Bereitschaft, 2.500–4.000 Euro für ein E-Bike auszugeben, ist gewachsen.

„Man muss die Vorteile herauskitzeln und das Produkt attraktiv machen. Das hat die E-Bike-Industrie geschafft, und ich glaube, dass unser Produkt dazu beigetragen hat", sagt Norbert nicht ohne Stolz. Durch die neue Gestaltung des Rahmens zum Beispiel. Norbert hat bewusst den klassischen Fahrradrahmen vermieden und einen kräftigen Aluminiumrahmen als tragendes Element gewählt. Motor und Batterien sind so gut integriert, dass sich eine eigene Erscheinung ergibt. „Mir ist ein ehrliches Gestaltungskonzept wichtig, eines, das wirklich auf den neuen Antrieb zugeschnitten ist. Der neue Antrieb braucht ein ansprechendes Design und sollte sich nicht als Staubsauger verkleiden."

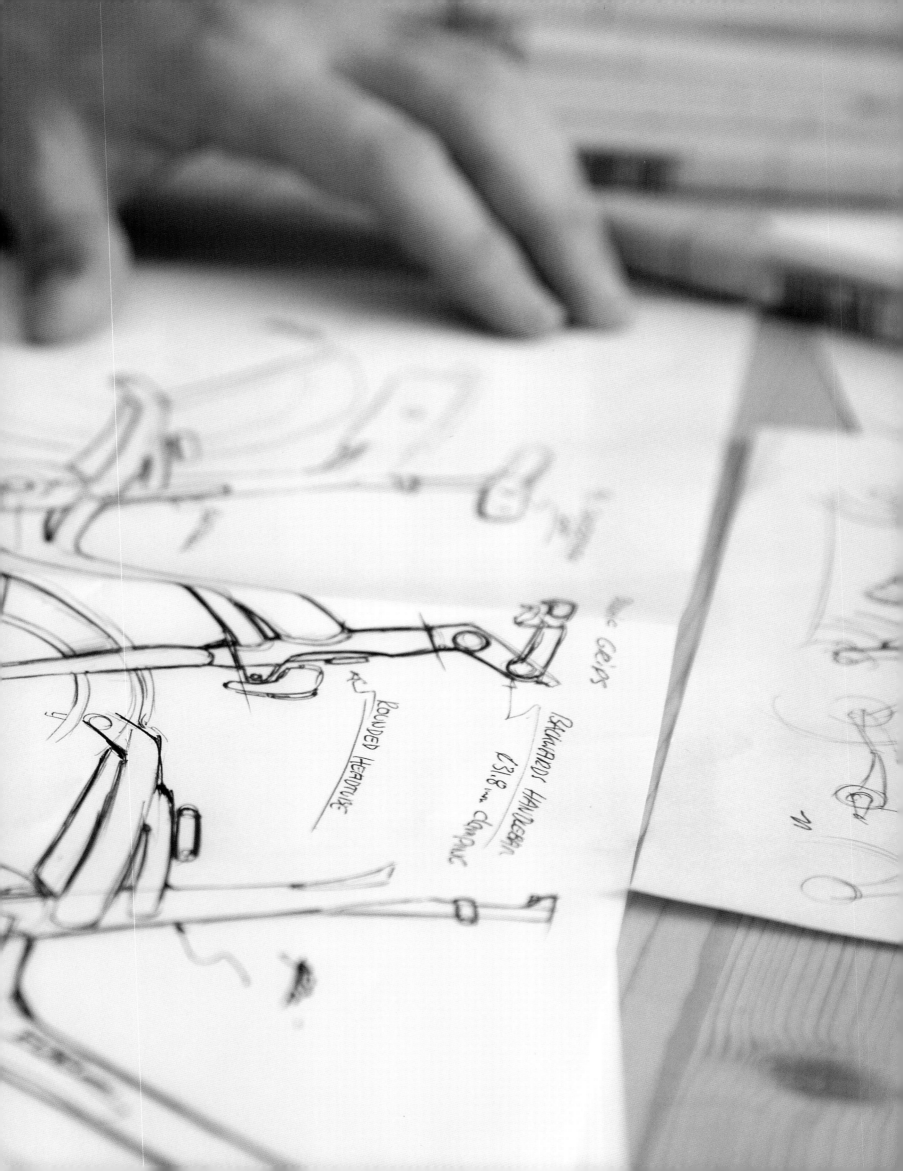

GENIE POWER

PORSCHE // HYBRID RS

The Hybrid RS from Porsche hearkens back to a surprisingly classic bicycle design. The four-bar suspension on the rear wheel as well as a telescopic fork with 4 inches travel on the front wheel give it the appearance of a normal mountain bike. But it is far from that. Many manufacturers use a discreet power design to integrate their batteries as inconspicuously as possible into the bike frame. But Porsche is nearly unmatched when it comes to the original way in which it camouflages its batteries: This sporty model in bright green hides its energy supply what seems to be a drinking bottle attached to the tube of the frame. When riding downhill, the drive motor switches over and generates power.

Mit dem Hybrid RS greift Porsche auf eine erstaunlich klassische Bikeform zurück. Die Viergelenkfederung am Hinterrad sowie eine Telegabel mit 100 Millimeter Federweg am Vorderrad lassen es wie ein normales Mountainbike erscheinen. Doch das ist es nicht. Viele Hersteller nutzen das sogenannte Hidden-Power-Design und bringen ihre Akkus möglichst unauffällig im Rahmen unter. Kaum jemand tarnt seine Akkus jedoch so originell wie Porsche: Das sportive Modell in Knallgrün versteckt seinen Energielieferanten in der am Rahmenrohr angebrachten Trinkflasche. Bei Bergabfahrten schaltet der Antriebsmotor um und wird zum Stromgenerator.

Country: Germany // Year: 2010 // Weight: 33 lb / 15 kg // Frame: carbon // Gears: 30-speed // Tires: 26"
Brakes: Magura Marta disc brakes // Battery: Lithium-Manganese // Type of drive: rear wheel hub motor 450 W
Max. range: 30 mi / 50 km // Design: Dr. Ing. h.c. F. Porsche AG

THE ULTIMATE
BIKING MACHINE

BMW // I PEDELEC CONCEPT

The new BMW i Pedelec Concept aims to be more than just a bike. It is an innovative interpretation of electro mobility for intermodal use in congested urban areas. It represents the ultimate companion to the BMW i3, the compact electric vehicle for urban areas that has been announced for a 2013 launch. Visually, this folding bike seems like a pair of scissors, and it functions in a similar way: In just a few easy steps, riders can quickly fold the aluminum and carbon fiber frame and then roll the bike along. Thanks to a crash-resistant mount, the BMW i3 Concept's trunk easily accommodates two folded pedelecs, which can be charged via the power outlet in the trunk.

Das neue BMW i Pedelec Concept will mehr sein als ein Bike. Es ist eine innovative Interpretation von Elektromobilität für den intermodalen Einsatz in Ballungsräumen und die ultimative Ergänzung zum BMW i3, dem kompakten Elektroauto für den urbanen Raum, das für 2013 angekündigt ist. Optisch wirkt das Faltrad wie eine Schere und so ähnlich funktioniert es auch: Der Rahmen aus Aluminium und Kohlefaser lässt sich durch Gelenke mit wenigen Handgriffen komprimieren und somit schieben. Zusammengefaltet finden zwei Pedelecs im Kofferraum des BMW i3 Concept mittels einer crashsicheren Haltevorrichtung Platz; über die Steckdose im Kofferraum können sie geladen werden.

Country: Germany // Year: small batch 2012 // Weight: 44 lb / 20 kg // Frame: aluminum and carbon fiber (50:50)
Gears: 3-speed hub gear // Tires: 16" // Brakes: front and rear hydraulic disc brakes
Battery: Lithium-Manganese 42 V 7.2 Ah 300 Wh // Type of drive: rear wheel hub motor 250 W
Max. range: 30 mi / 50 km // Speed: 15 mph / 25 km/h // Design: BMW

STUNT BIKE

AUDI // AUDI E-BIKE WÖRTHERSEE

The annual event at Wörthersee introduces sporty little numbers and unusual vehicles, which is how this show and stunt bike comes by its unusual name. But the name quickly fades into the background, once the electric motor starts supplying an impressive 2.3 kilowatts. With that output, the e-bike can reach speeds of up to 50 miles per hour, and the rear wheel can achieve torques of up to 185 pound-force feet. The bike is manufactured from carbon fiber reinforced plastic and features five riding modes: a "pure" mode, for human-powered-only riding for the rare occasion that the motor might break down; a "pedelec" mode that offers electrical assistance; an "eGrip" electric-only mode; and a "balanced wheelie" mode. For stunt and trick riders, the Wörthersee prototype additionally offers a "power wheelie" mode that allows riding on the rear wheel.

Auf dem Wörtherseetreffen werden jährlich heiße Flitzer und außergewöhnliche Fahrzeuge vorgestellt. So kommt das sportliche Trial- und Stuntbike zu seinem ungewöhnlichen Namen. Aber der gerät schnell in Vergessenheit: Der Elektromotor leistet beeindruckende 2,3 Kilowatt. Damit können bis zu 80 Kilometer pro Stunde erreicht werden und das Hinterrad schafft es auf bis zu 250 Newtonmeter Drehmoment. Das Bike ist aus kohlenstofffaserverstärktem Kunststoff gefertigt und bietet stolze fünf Fahrmodi: einen Pure-Modus zum Antrieb mit Muskelkraft, für den Fall, dass der Motor einmal schlapp macht, einen Pedelec-Modus zur elektrischen Unterstützung, einen eGrip-Modus zum rein elektrischen Antrieb und einen Balanced-Wheelie-Modus zur gesteuerten Haltung des Gleichgewichts. Für Stuntfahrer und Trickkünstler verfügt der Prototyp zudem über einen Power-Wheelie-Modus, der Fahrspaß auf dem Hinterrad ermöglicht.

Country: Germany // Year: presented in 2012 // Weight: 46 lb / 21 kg // Frame: carbon
Gears: 9-speed hydraulic derailleur // Tires: 26" // Brakes: Brake Force One hydraulic disc brakes
Battery: TQ-System / Clean Mobile Lithium-Ion 48 V 11 Ah 530 Wh // Type of drive: center motor 2,300 W
Max. range: 45 mi / 70 km // Speed: 50 mph / 80 km/h // Design: Wolfgang Egger, Hendrik Schaefers

UNISEX POWER

FORD // E-BIKE CONCEPT

||||||||||||||||||||||||||||||||||||||||||||||||||||||||||||||||||||||||||||||||||||||||||||||

What makes the e-bike from Ford-Werke fascinating is its powerful lithium-ion battery integrated into the rugged trapezoidal frame, which weighs in at a mere 5.5 pounds. The Ford design team joined forces with cyber-Wear Heidelberg GmbH to create the bicycle's sporty yet minimalistic appearance. The E-Bike Concept was designed for both women and men, which explains the low step-through frame. Instead of a derailleur, this e-bike features a belt drive system that ensures a clean transfer of energy. There are currently no plans for mass production.

Das E-Bike der Ford-Werke besticht durch seine leistungsfähige Lithium-Ionen-Batterie, die im robusten trapez-förmigen Rahmen integriert ist. Dieser bringt gerade einmal 2,5 Kilogramm auf die Waage. Für die sportliche, minimalistische Optik des Rads sind das Ford-Design-Team und die cyber-Wear Heidelberg GmbH verantwortlich. Entwickelt wurde das E-Bike Concept sowohl für Frauen als auch für Männer, was den tiefen Einstieg erklärt. Anstelle einer Kettenschaltung hat es einen Riemenantrieb, wodurch eine saubere Kraftübertragung sichergestellt ist. Eine Serienproduktion ist allerdings bisher nicht geplant.

Country: Germany // Year: 2011 // Frame: aluminum and carbon // Gears: 11-speed Shimano Alfine hub gear
Tires: 28" // Brakes: Avid Elixir 5 hydraulic disc brakes // Battery: Lithium-Ion 36 V 9.3 Ah 335 Wh
Type of drive: front wheel hub motor 350 W // Max. range: 55 mi / 85 km // Speed: 15 mph / 25 km/h
Design: Ford Europe design team / cyber-Wear Heidelberg GmbH

THE COMMUNICATOR

TOYOTA // PAS WITH

Toyota has enjoyed a long business relationship with Yamaha Motor. The creative forces at the two companies are working together on a new generation of vehicles that are capable of communicating with other means of transportation and their environment. According to information from the manufacturer, the Pas With e-bike will be equipped with a display attached to the frame that will be linked to the Toyota Smart Center, a power management network. The display provides riders with information regarding the vehicle's status and the closest charging station. This e-bike is expected to support vehicle sharing, a feature which makes it possible to manage vehicles shared with other users.

Toyota und Yamaha Motor verbindet eine lange Geschäftsbeziehung. Derweil arbeiten die kreativen Köpfe der beiden Konzerne an einer neuen Generation von Fahrzeugen, die in der Lage sind, mit anderen Verkehrsmitteln und der Umgebung zu kommunizieren. Nach Herstellerangaben soll das E-Bike Pas With mit einem am Rahmen befestigten Display ausgestattet sein, das mit dem Toyota Smart Center, einem Strom-Management-System, verbunden ist. Darüber erhält der Fahrer zum Beispiel Informationen zum Zustand des Fahrzeugs und zur nächstgelegene Strom-ladestation. Auch eine Verwaltung von Fahrzeugen, die mit anderen zusammen genutzt werden („Vehicle Sharing"), soll mit dem E-Bike möglich sein.

Country: Japan // Year: presented in 2011 // Weight: 44 lb / 20 kg // Max. range: 30 mi / 45 km

1928 REVIVAL

OPEL // RAD E

"Sculptural artistry meets German precision," has been Opel's design philosophy for over 150 years. Opel's latest contribution to electromobility, the RAD e, adheres to this philosophy with its "boomerang" styling elements. Instead of the lightweight construction so typical of many e-bikes, the frame of the RAD e is made of hollow pressed steel. Opel used this material back in the late 1920s for its legendary Motoclub 500 motorcycle, revolutionizing production by significantly reducing manufacturing times. The futuristic RAD e is controlled by a smartphone. If you happen to have an Opel with a FlexFix bicycle carrier system, the e-bike can even be charged while being transported by car.

„Skulpturale Eleganz trifft deutsche Ingenieurskunst", so lautet die Design-Philosophie von Opel seit über 150 Jahren. Auch das RAD e, Opels neuester Beitrag zur Elektromobilität, gehorcht mit seinen bumerangförmigen Stil-elementen dieser Maxime. Anstelle der für viele E-Bikes typischen Leichtbaumaterialien besteht der Rahmen aus hohlem Pressstahl. Dieses Material wurde von Opel schon in den späten 20er-Jahren für das legendäre Motorrad Motoclub 500 verwendet und revolutionierte damals die Produktion, vor allem durch deutlich verkürzte Herstellungs-zeiten. Gesteuert wird das futuristische Gefährt über ein Smartphone. Wer zudem noch einen Opel mit FlexFix-Fahrradträger fährt, kann das E-Bike sogar während der Autofahrt laden.

Country: Germany // Year: 2012 // Weight: 42 lb / 19 kg // Frame: steel // Gears: 22-speed // Tires: 28"
Brakes: disc brakes // Battery: Lithium-Ion // Type of drive: center motor 250 W // Max. range: 85 mi / 140 km
Speed: 15 mph / 25 km/h // Design: Opel Design Team

KEEPS GOING

MOVE CONTROL TEAM, POLITECNICO DI MILANO // BIKE+

Genius Leonardo da Vinci not only invented the planetary gear installed in some e-bike gear systems, he also made sketches for a perpetual motion machine. Inspired by these ideas, his "descendants" at the Politecnico di Milano built the Bike+, the only bike to date that never has to be plugged in to be charged. Instead, the rider charges the battery by gently and lightly pedaling and braking. The motor provides assistance when the rider begins to pedal inefficiently or with difficulty. This technology reduces the effort while riding and the bike retains its 100% zero emissions rating.

Universalgenie Leonardo da Vinci hat nicht nur das in einigen E-Bike-Schaltungen verbaute Planetengetriebe erfunden, sondern auch Skizzen für ein Perpetuum mobile entworfen. Seine „Nachfahren" vom Politecnico di Milano haben ihm nachgeeifert und mit dem Bike+ das bisher einzige E-Bike gebaut, das niemals wieder an der Steckdose aufgeladen werden muss. Die Batterien werden aufgeladen, wenn sanft und leicht in die Pedale getreten und gebremst wird, und der Fahrer wird dann unterstützt, wenn das Treten in die Pedale beschwerlich und ineffizient ist. So reduziert sich die Anstrengung beim Fahren und das Rad bleibt trotzdem zu 100 Prozent emissionsfrei.

Country: Italy // Year: presented in 2011 // Weight: 32.6 lb / 14.8 kg // Frame: carbon
Gears: 11-speed Shimano Alfine // Tires: 28" // Brakes: Shimano Alfine hydraulic disc brakes
Battery: Lithium-Ion 36 V 2.2 Ah 80 Wh // Type of drive: CUTE Front geared hub drive 250 W
Max. range: in bike+ mode: "infinite" // Speed: 15 mph / 25 km/h // Design: Fabio Ferri, Giovanni Alli

ON THE GO

YUJI FUJIMURA // EBIQ

||||||||||||||||||||||||||||||||||||||||||||||||||||||||||||||||||

Although the Ebiq is only a concept, it is a fascinating one—and could be a dream come true for busy people who are constantly running late. Your cell phone needs to be charged, your laptop's battery is so low that it won't even turn on, and you have to leave the house in a hurry? No problem, because the battery on the Ebiq can charge them all. Using the integrated display that can be connected to your laptop or smartphone, you can even stay abreast of events as you ride through the city. Once you get home, you simply fold in the handlebars and saddle and slide the bike into the narrow gap between a wall and a cabinet.

Zwar ist das Ebiq bisher nur eine Vision, dafür aber eine faszinierende und ein wahrer Traum für verplante Zuspät-kommer. Das Handy bettelt um Strom, der Laptop ist so leer, dass er sich nicht mehr einschalten lässt, und man muss fluchtartig das Haus verlassen? Kein Problem, denn die Batterie des Ebiq lädt sie auf. Durch den eingebauten Screen, der mit dem Laptop oder Smartphone verbunden werden kann, ist man sogar während der Fahrt in der City immer auf dem Laufenden. Zu Hause angekommen, klappt man Lenker und Sattel einfach ein und schiebt das Rad in den schmalen Spalt zwischen Wand und Schrank.

Country: Japan // Weight: 66 lb / 30 kg // Frame: aluminum // Tires: 20" // Battery: Lithium-Ion
Speed: over 6 mph / 10 km/h, less than 15 mph / 25 km/h // Design: Yuji Fujimura

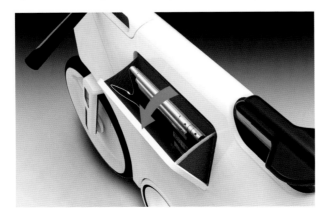

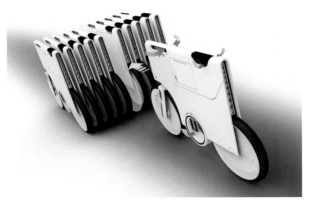

RED DOT

MIT SENSEABLE CITY LAB // COPENHAGEN WHEEL

This stylish wheel with the red hub was developed by researchers at the Massachusetts Institute of Technology. Introduced at the 2009 UN Climate Conference, the bike is representative of efforts underway to make Copenhagen the first climate-neutral capital in the world by 2025. The red housing surrounding the hub conceals the electronics along with environmental data storage, all taking up minimal space. The wheel captures the energy from braking and stores it for when you need a boost. And there's a special touch: You can use your smartphone to control the Copenhagen Wheel and regulate the level of motor assistance you would like.

Entwickelt wurde das schicke Rad mit dem roten Hingucker von Forschern am Massachusetts Institute of Technology. Das auf der UN-Klimakonferenz 2009 vorgestellte Bike steht ganz im Zeichen der Bemühungen, Kopenhagen bis 2025 zur ersten klimaneutralen Hauptstadt der Welt zu machen. Die Elektronik samt Umweltdatenspeicher verbirgt sich in dem roten Gehäuse an der Nabe und ist auf ein Minimum reduziert. Beim Rückwärtstreten bremst das Rad und speichert die Energie, die bei Bedarf in Antriebskraft umgesetzt wird. Besonderer Clou: Mit dem Smartphone lässt sich das Copenhagen Wheel steuern und die Unterstützungsstärke regulieren.

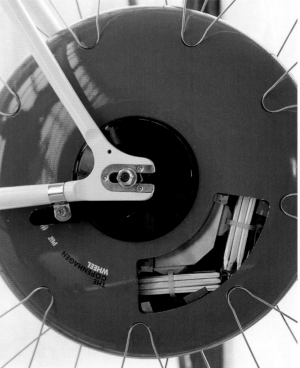

Country: USA // Battery: Lithium-Ion

RIGHT BIKE FOR YOUR TYPE

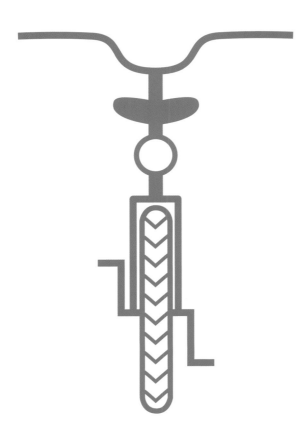

BIKERS WITH BENEFITS

EASY PEDELEC

Are you a cyclist who could do with just a little help? Then Easy Pedelecs are perfect for you! Visually speaking, these models strongly reference classic bicycles. The batteries are frequently concealed in the frame. Above all else, these bikes are comfortable, not too flashy and come equipped with a rack or panniers. They are easy to operate and maintain and are perfect for running errands, commuting comfortably, visits, and short outings. Plus they will put a big smile on your face, because regardless of whether you're heading uphill, just starting off, or reaching the end of your ride, it will feel as if you're being gently pushed by an invisible hand.

Sie sind Fahrradfahrer und wünschen sich das gewisse Extra? Dann sind Sie der Typ für Easy Pedelecs. Die Modelle lehnen sich optisch stark an das klassische Fahrrad an. Oft sind die Akkus im Rahmen versteckt. Diese Räder sind vor allem bequem und nicht zu extravagant, haben einen Gepäckträger oder Satteltaschen. Sie sind leicht in der Bedienung und der Pflege und eignen sich für Besorgungen, gemütliches Pendeln, Besuche und kleinere Ausflüge. Und sie zaubern Ihnen dieses „Alles ist gut"-Lächeln ins Gesicht. Denn bergauf, beim Anfahren und auf den letzten Kilometern werden Sie wie von Zauberhand angeschoben.

PENCIL PUSHERS

COMFORT PEDELEC

You commute to work, you have a place to store and charge your bike there, and you care about your image and how you look? These intelligently designed bikes that come equipped with a rack will be a very good fit for you. You can even choose an e-bike that is operated without the classic chain—no more greasy pant legs and naked shins. In other words, this is a business-class bicycle.

Sie sind Berufspendler, haben eine Abstell- und Auflademöglichkeit am Arbeitsplatz und achten auf Ihr Image und Ihr Äußeres? Dann sind Sie mit durchdesignten Rädern mit Gepäckträger gut bedient. Dazu gibt es E-Bikes, die ohne klassische Kette betrieben werden. Das ist das Ende von verschmierten Hosenbeinen und entblößten Waden. Ein Rad der Businessclass.

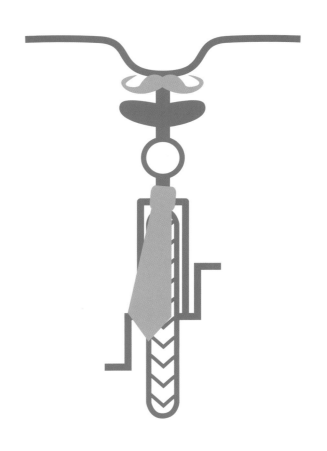

DELIVERY SERVICES

TRANSPORT PEDELEC

Do you often carry a heavy load? Whether you do so for your professional or personal life, you need an e-bike with plenty of cargo space and strong batteries, equipped with thick tires, reliable brakes, and stable wheels. Whether you're transporting moving boxes or a mountain of empty bottles from your last party, or running an errand to the post office, you'll be able to move plenty of cargo from point A to point B—without muscle cramps in your arms and legs and a stiff neck and shoulders.

Sie haben immer viel zu transportieren? Ob beruflich oder privat, sie brauchen ein E-Bike mit viel Ladefläche und starken Akkus, mit dicken Reifen, zuverlässigen Bremsen und mehreren stabilen Rädern. Von Umzugskisten über Leergutberge der letzten Party bis zur Post lässt sich hier viel von A nach B schaffen. Ohne Muskelkater in den Armen und Beinen und Verspannungen in Schultern und Nacken.

THE MAMAS & THE PAPAS

FAMILY PEDELEC

Are you a hip, environmentally aware parent, or do you work as a nursery school teacher? Perhaps you're not sure how to transport more than two children at a time without your muscles cramping up on the way to the playground? Even if you don't have little ones clinging to the hem of your skirt, maybe you're trying to figure out how on earth you're going to get that crate of organic apple juice, milk, and potatoes home from the store without throwing out your back? Cargo bikes are great for young families who may not have long distances to cover, but often have plenty to transport.

Sie sind junge, umweltbewusste Eltern oder von Beruf Kindergärtner? Sie wissen manchmal nicht, wie sie mehr als zwei Kinder emissionslos auf einmal befördern sollen, ohne schon auf dem Hinweg zum Spielplatz den Muskelkater des nächsten Morgens zu ahnen? Und selbst wenn die Kleinen nicht an Ihrem Rockzipfel hängen, überlegen Sie verzweifelt, wie Sie den Kasten naturtrüben Apfelsaft, die Landmilch und die Bio-kartoffeln ohne Bandscheibenvorfall vom Laden nach Hause bekommen? Transportfreudige Räder sind toll für junge Familien, die sich nicht weit, aber oft mit Last bewegen.

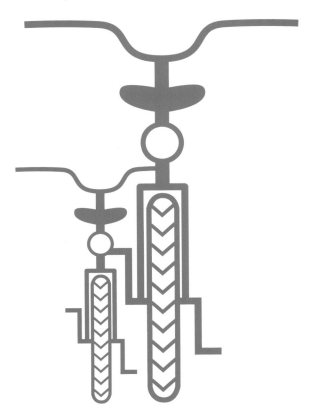

NATURE LOVERS

WELLNESS PEDELEC

Do you love the outdoors and enjoy being active, but you don't want to play a competitive sport? Do you feel it is important not to harm the environment? Just imagine if you had a quiet motor that would enable you to quickly and easily go on long rides without being worn out. These bikes are comfortable, the batteries have a good range, and they provide plenty of places to stow your gear.

Sie lieben die Natur und haben Freude an Bewegung, wollen allerdings keinen Leistungssport betreiben? Sie legen Wert darauf, dabei der Umwelt nicht zu schaden? Stellen Sie sich vor, mithilfe eines leisen Motors schnell und einfach lange Touren mit Raffinesse zu bewältigen. Die Touren-Bikes sind bequem, haben eine ausdauernde Batterie und lassen genug Möglichkeiten, das Reisegepäck zu verstauen.

STYLISH ATHLETES

SPORT PEDELEC

Do you live by the motto "harder, better, faster, stronger," but you still sometimes reach your physical limits? A motorized mountain bike will enable you to push those limits even further. E-bikes undermine sports morale? Just the opposite! They will egg you on to venture into unknown terrain. You'll be able to tackle even steeper mountainsides and go downhill faster than ever.

„Harder, better, faster, stronger" ist Ihr Motto? Aber irgendwann stoßen Sie an Ihre körperlichen Grenzen? Mit einem motorisierten Mountainbike verschieben Sie diese Grenzen noch einmal. E-Bikes untergraben die Sportmoral? Keineswegs, hier stacheln sie an, sich in unbekanntes Terrain vorzuwagen. Damit geht es in den Bergen noch steiler hinauf und downhill wird es noch rasanter.

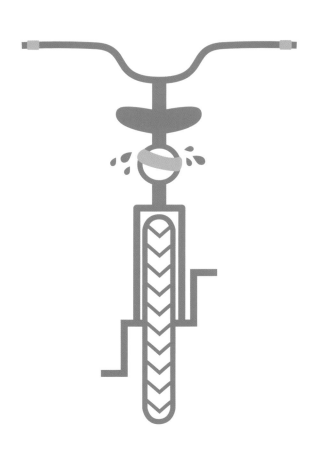

BRAVE-HEARTS

REHA PEDELEC

Rehabilitation pedelecs combine a means of transport with physiotherapy. Handbikes restore mobility to individuals who have lost the use of their legs. Cardio bikes that are controlled via heart rate can help patients regain their fitness after a surgery or stroke, all without overexerting themselves. E-bikes are ideal for helping almost anyone regain mobility and participate in everyday life.

Reha Pedelecs sind eine Mischung aus Fortbewegungsmittel und Trainingsgerät. Handbikes geben Menschen, die ihre Beine nicht mehr benutzen können, ein Stück Mobilität zurück. Cardiobikes, die via Herzfrequenz gesteuert werden, helfen Patienten nach Operationen oder Schlaganfällen, wieder Kondition aufzubauen, ohne sich zu überanstrengen. E-Bikes sind wie geschaffen dafür, fast jeden Menschen wieder mobil zu machen und am alltäglichen Leben teilhaben zu lassen.

FLEXIBLE COMMUTERS

FOLDABLE PEDELEC

Hybrid vehicles are very hip right now. So is a new genre of big city residents: hybrid commuters. They use both public and private transportation for their daily commute. Apart from unrestricted mobility, flexibility is of utmost importance to them. These small foldable vehicles are ideal city bikes that you can easily take with you onto the subway or into a taxi. And once you reach your destination, they will fit under any table.

Hybridfahrzeuge sind im Trend. Aber nicht nur sie, sondern auch eine neue Gattung von Großstadtbewohnern: der Hybridpendler. Er legt seine täglichen Wegstrecken halb mit den Öffentlichen, halb mit einem privaten Verkehrsmittel zurück. Neben uneingeschränkter Mobilität ist Flexibilität oberstes Gebot. Diese kleinen faltbaren Flitzer sind ideale Citybikes, die man mit in die Metro oder ins Taxi nehmen kann und die am Zielort unter jeden Tisch passen.

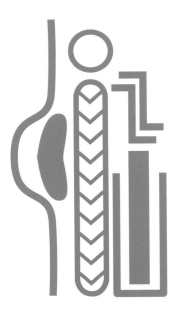

GLOSSARY

AH → (short for ampere-hour) describes the charge available. The capacity of the → battery is the maximum available amount of charge. But without also knowing the voltage → V (Volts) Ah isn't an absolute quantity. The actual energy available is better expressed in → Wh (watt-hours).

BATSO → stands for Battery Safety Organization. The BATSO safety standard was first developed in 2002 and includes testing for transport and use. This makes it the highest available standard. Since May 2012, it's on its way to becoming an EN standard. www.batso.org

BATTERY → Storage for electrical energy. Often used as synonymous with → battery pack. On → pedelecs the batteries are the single most expensive component. Batteries differ in size, chemistry, and weight.

BATTERY PACK → A complete unit for energy storage, consisting of many individual parts, assembled into a "pack" and packaged in a housing together with the → power electronics.

BMS → (short for Battery Management System). → Power electronics which are built into the → battery pack ensure that the cells are kept in the best possible condition so that the battery lasts as long as possible. In addition, a BMS can provide information such as the number of → charge cycles, current charge status, battery health status, and expected remaining service life via an electronic communications protocol such as → EnergyBus.

CENTER MOTOR → A motor built into the frame or attached to the bottom bracket (crank motor), which drives via the chain. Generally requires a specially designed frame.

CHARGE CYCLE → Discharging and then charging a → battery (100 %), which could consist of several partial charges (e. g. 4 × 25 %). What counts is the energy added. A specification of, for example, 500 charge cycles means that the battery can be 100 % recharged at least 500 times and will still retain the minimum remaining capacity as specified by the manufacturer (generally 85 % of the capacity when new).

CONNECTORS → These are releasable electrical connection elements and are used in the manufacture of power and data cable connections. The most commonly used connector plug on → LEVs is in general the charger plug. Often however, the pins on identical-looking plugs are differently configured, which can inadvertently lead to incompatible → batteries and chargers being connected together. This can result in a dangerous situation which could have been avoided.

E-BIKE 45 → A (usually) two-wheeled vehicle with an electric motor that can also function independently without pedalling (completely electrically powered). E-Bike 45s are treated in Germany as → small powered bikes for which insurance is mandatory. If power assistance is limited to 12 mph (E-Bike 20), they can be ridden without a helmet.

ELECTRIC BIKE → Widely used umbrella term for → Pedelec 25s, → Pedelec 45s, E-Bike 20s and → E-Bike 45s.

ENERGYBUS STANDARD → An open standard developed since 2002 by the membership organization EnergyBus e. V. for the electrical components of → LEVs. Consists of a connector family and a communication protocol based around the CANopen industrial machine language. Power transfer is combined with data communication. In March 2011 the protocol between → battery and charger was released, and in March 2012 that for the standardized connector. www.energybus.org

ENERGY DENSITY → is a measure referring to → the amount of energy a battery can store, and which can then be made available per unit of volume or weight. There are batteries which are optimized for maximum capacity per unit volume or weight, others for maximum power delivery per unit of volume or weight. Energy density also applies to drive systems, where it is the deliverable power of the drive per unit volume or weight.

E-SCOOTER → A purely electric vehicle without pedals, similar to a roller. E-Scooters are → small powered bikes and insurance is mandatory.

FRONT HUB MOTOR → Motor in the hub of the front wheel. Its greatest advantage is the ease of fitting and compatibility with any sort of gear hub or coaster brake.

HUB MOTOR → A motor which is fitted at the hub of either the front or rear wheel.

HYBRID VEHICLE → A vehicle driven by a mix of at least two types of drive. For a → pedelec this refers to the combination of human muscle power and an electric motor. For cars labelled "hybrid" this usually refers to the combination of electric and internal combustion motors.

LEV → (short for Light Electric Vehicle). Umbrella term for electrically driven lightweight vehicles such as → pedelecs, but also E-Wheelchairs, E-Lawnmowers etc.

LI-ION BATTERY → A battery with lithium chemistry. Lithium is currently used in almost all commercial systems, because lithium technology has advantages over other types, including holding more energy per unit weight and volume.

MEMORY EFFECT → An effect which occurs primarily in nickel-based → batteries. It happens when the battery is "top up" charged, before it is empty. The battery "remembers" the level from which it was charged and then "expects" a recharge at that level, so it only provides energy until that previous recharge level is reached. This effect does not occur on batteries with Lithium chemistry (→ Li-Ion battery).

MOTOR CONTROLLER → Power electronics for controlling the motor power output.

PEDELEC 25 → (from Pedal Electric Cycle). By far the most widespread form of → electric bike. The motor only provides assistance while you are pedaling. If the motor assist is limited to 15 mph and the motor power rating is no higher than 250 W, then it is treated the same as a bicycle within the EU. You can ride it without a helmet or proof of insurance, and can ride on cycle paths. Was patented in 1982 by Egon Gelhard and first sold in 1992 by Yamaha in Japan.

PEDELEC 45 → A fast pedelec, whose motor assists while pedaling over 15 mph up to a maximum of 28 mph. Needs type approval as a → small powered bike and accordingly also requires proof of insurance. Some Pedelec 45s have a control, e. g., a twist grip throttle, with which they can be ridden on a purely electrical basis up to 12 mph.

POWER ELECTRONICS → Nowadays the high currents in chargers and motor controllers are controlled as needed by power electronics.

PUSH ASSIST → This is mostly activated via a button, more rarely via a twist grip. It propels the → pedelec up to 13 mph (a legal limit) without any need for pedaling. It's handy on ramps or when walking uphill. In Germany riding vehicles with push assist requires either a driving license or a moped test certificate.

RANGE → means the distance in miles which can be covered wit h motor power. Often given by manufacturers as an absolute (estimated) number. The actual range is relative and depends on factors including terrain and riding style.

REAR DRIVE → Typically a hub motor in the rear wheel. Can be combined with a derailleur transmission or integrated with hub gears.

REGENERATION RETURNING → Energy from braking to the → battery. Some drive systems switch the motor into a generator mode when braking. Currently this can extend the range by around 10 %.

ROTATION SENSOR → Used in→ pedelecs of simpler construction. Measures pedal motion at the bottom bracket and, when the pedals are turning, enables the electric drive.

SMALL POWERED BIKE → A motorized two-wheeler with a top speed limited by design to 28 mph (since driving license reform 1998/99). Can carry two people when designed to do so.

TORQUE → The force which a drive system exerts in a turning action (whether on pedals or wheel rotation). Given in Newton meters (Nm), and is an indication of the assistance force available.

TORQUE SENSOR → Most → pedelecs in the price bracket above 2,000 dollars have a torque sensor which measures the applied muscle power very accurately, and so enables the motor controller to apply motor power in proportion to the pedaling effort applied.

V → (short for Volts). Unit of electrical potential. For → pedelecs, nominal voltages of 24, 26, 32, 36 and 48 V are typical.

WH → (short for watt-hours). The actual energy capacity of a → battery. The product of charge (→ Ah) and voltage (→ V). A 36 V battery with 10 Ah capacity will deliver 360 Wh (36 V × 10 Ah) of energy.

AH → (kurz für Amperestunde) gibt die verfügbare Ladung an. Die Kapazität der → Batterie entspricht der maximal verfügbaren Ladungsmenge. Diese ist ohne die Angabe der Spannung → V (Volt) kein absoluter Mengenwert. Die tatsächlich verfügbare Energiemenge wird daher besser in → Wh (Wattstunde) angegeben.

AKKUMULATOR → (kurz Akku). Speicher für elektrische Energie. Oft synonym mit → Batterie verwendet. An → Pedelecs sind Akkus die teuersten Einzelbauteile. Sie unterscheiden sich in Größe, Chemie und Gewicht.

BATSO → steht für Battery Safety Organization. Der Sicherheitsstandard BATSO wurde seit 2002 entwickelt und enthält Prüfungen zum Transport und Gebrauch. Er ist damit der höchste verfügbare Standard. Seit Mai 2012 auf dem Weg zur EN-Norm. www.batso.org

BATTERIE → Kompakte Einheit zur Energiespeicherung; besteht aus vielen Einzelzellen, die zu einem „Pack" zusammengefasst und mit der → Leistungselektronik in einem Gehäuse untergebracht sind.

BEWEGUNGSSENSOR → Verwendet an Pedelecs der einfacheren Bauart. Misst die Pedalbewegung am Tretlager und gibt bei Trittbewegung den Elektroantrieb frei.

BMS → (kurz für Batterie Management System). → Leistungselektronik, die in die Batterie integriert ist und dafür sorgt, dass der Zustand der Zellen möglichst gut ist und damit die Batterie so lange wie möglich lebt. Des Weiteren kann ein BMS über eine elektronische Kommunikationssprache, beispielsweise → EnergyBus, Informationen zur Nutzungshistorie wie die Anzahl der Ladezyklen, den aktuellen Ladezustand, den Gesundheitszustand und die voraussichtliche Restlebensdauer herausgeben.

DREHMOMENT → Die Kraft, die ein Antrieb auf eine Drehbewegung (wie Pedal- oder Raddrehung) ausübt. Wird in Newtonmeter (Nm) angegeben und ist ein Indikator für die verfügbare Unterstützungskraft.

E-BIKE 45 → (Meist) zweirädriges Gefährt mit Elektromotor, der auch unabhängig vom Treten funktioniert (rein elektrisch). E-Bikes gelten in Deutschland als zulassungspflichtige → Kleinkrafträder. Ist die Unterstützung auf 20 Kilometer pro Stunde beschränkt (E-Bike 20), dürfen sie ohne Helm gefahren werden.

ELEKTROFAHRRAD → Häufig verwendeter Oberbegriff für → Pedelecs 25, → Pedelecs 45, E-Bikes 20 und → E-Bikes 45.

ENERGIEDICHTE → Bei → Batterien die Energie, die je Volumen und Gewichtseinheit gespeichert werden kann und verfügbar ist. Es gibt Batterien, die auf maximale Kapazität pro Volumen je Gewicht optimiert sind, andere auf maximale Stromentnahme pro Volumen je Gewicht. Der Begriff wird auch bei Antrieben verwendet. Dort ist es die verfügbare Leistung eines Antriebs je Volumen je Gewichtseinheit.

ENERGYBUS-STANDARD → Seit 2002 von der Mitgliederorganisation EnergyBus e. V. entwickelter offener Standard für die elektrischen Komponenten von → LEVs. Besteht aus einer Steckerfamilie und einem auf der Maschinensprache CANopen basierenden Kommunikationsprotokoll. Die Leistungsübertragung ist gekoppelt mit der Datenkommunikation. Im März 2011 wurde das Protokoll zwischen Batterie und Ladegerät freigegeben und im März 2012 der genormte Ladestecker. www.energybus.org

E-SCOOTER → Reine Elektrofahrzeuge ohne Pedale, oft Rollern ähnlich. E-Scooter sind → Kleinkrafträder und zulassungspflichtig.

FRONTNABENMOTOR → Motor in der Nabe des Vorderrads. Größte Stärken sind die einfache Nachrüstung und die Kombinierbarkeit mit jeder Gangschaltung und Rücktrittbremse.

HECKANTRIEB → Typischerweise ein Nabenmotor im Hinterrad. Kann mit einer Kettenschaltung kombiniert oder in eine Nabenschaltung integriert werden.

HYBRIDFAHRZEUG → Fahrzeug, das mit einem Mix aus mindestens zwei Antriebsarten betrieben wird. Beim → Pedelec sind das menschliche Muskelkraft und Elektromotor. Bei Autos bezeichnet »Hybrid« meist die Kombination aus Elektro- und Verbrennungsmotor.

KLEINKRAFTRAD → Motorisiertes Zweirad mit einer bauartbedingten Höchstgeschwindigkeit von 45 Kilometern pro Stunde (seit Führerscheinreform 1998/99). Kann zwei Personen befördern, wenn dafür konstruiert.

KRAFTSENSOR → Die meisten → Pedelecs im Preisbereich ab 1.500 Euro haben einen Kraftsensor, der die Muskelkraft sehr präzise misst und so der Motorsteuerung ermöglicht, die Motorkraft in Relation zur aufgebrachten Trittkraft dazuzugeben.

LADEZYKLUS → Entladung und anschließende Ladung eines → Akkus (100 Prozent), kann mehrere Teilladungen (zum Beispiel 4 × 25 Prozent) umfassen – was zählt, ist die nachgeladene Energie. Angaben von beispielsweise 500 Ladezyklen bedeuten, dass der Akku mindestens 500 mal zu 100 Prozent aufgeladen werden kann und dabei noch mindestens die vom Hersteller spezifizierte Restkapazität hat (meist 85 Prozent der Speicherfähigkeit des Neuzustands).

LEISTUNGSELEKTRONIK → Heute werden in Ladegeräten und Motorsteuerungen hohe Ströme mittels Leistungselektronik entsprechend dosiert.

LEV → (kurz für Light Electric Vehicle, Leicht-Elektro-Fahrzeug). Oberbegriff für elektrisch angetriebene Leichtfahrzeuge wie → Pedelecs, aber auch E-Rollstühle, E-Rasenmäher etc.

LI-IONEN-AKKU → Akku auf der Basis von Lithium. Lithium wird gegenwärtig in fast allen gängigen Systemen eingesetzt, da die Lithium-Technologie gegenüber anderen Vorteile aufweist, wie beispielsweise mehr Energie je Volumen und Gewichtseinheit.

MEMORYEFFEKT → Vor allem bei Akkus auf der Basis von Nickel auftretender Effekt, der eintritt, wenn der → Akku zwischengeladen wird, ohne leer gewesen zu sein. Der Akku „merkt" sich das Niveau, ab dem er geladen wurde, und „erwartet" künftig von da an eine Neuladung, das heißt, er gibt Energie nur noch bis zu diesem Level ab. Bei Akkus auf der Basis von Lithium (→ Li-Ion-Akku) tritt der Effekt nicht auf.

MITTELMOTOR → In den Rahmen integrierter bzw. im Tretlager untergebrachter Motor (Tretlagermotor), der über die Kette wirkt. Erfordert meist einen speziell dafür konstruierten Rahmen.

MOTORSTEUERUNG → Leistungselektronik zur Dosierung der Motorkraft.

NABENMOTOR → Motor, der in der Nabe des Vorder- oder Hinterrads untergebracht ist.

PEDELEC 25 → (von Pedal Electric Cycle). Am weitesten verbreitete Art von → Elektrofahrrädern. Der Motor unterstützt nur, wenn getreten wird. Ist die Motorunterstützung auf 25 Kilometer pro Stunde begrenzt und die Motornennleistung nicht höher als 250 Watt, sind Pedelecs 25 in der EU Fahrrädern gleichgestellt. Sie dürfen damit ohne Helm, ohne Versicherungskennzeichen und auf dem Fahrradweg gefahren werden.

Wurden 1982 von Egon Gelhard patentiert und 1992 erstmals von Yamaha in Japan verkauft.

PEDELEC 45 → Schnelles Pedelec. Der Motor unterstützt beim Treten über 25 Kilometer pro Stunde hinaus, bis maximal 45 Kilometer pro Stunde. Braucht eine Straßenzulassung als Kleinkraftrad und damit ein Versicherungskennzeichen. Einige Pedelecs 45 besitzen eine Vorrichtung, zum Beispiel einen Gasgriff, mit dem bis zu 20 Kilometern pro Stunde rein elektrisch gefahren werden kann.

REICHWEITE → Gibt die Strecke in Kilometern an, die mit Motorkraft zurückgelegt werden kann. Wird von Herstellern oft als absoluter (Schätz-)Wert angegeben. Die tatsächliche Reichweite ist relativ und beispielsweise abhängig von Geländeart und Fahrverhalten.

REKUPERATION → Rückspeisung von Bremsenergie in den → Akku. Manche Antriebe können den Antriebsmotor beim Bremsen in einen Generatormodus umschalten. Die Reichweite kann damit aktuell um rund zehn Prozent gesteigert werden.

SCHIEBEHILFE → Wird meist auf Knopfdruck, seltener mit Drehgriff aktiviert. Beschleunigt das → Pedelec auf bis zu sechs Kilometer pro Stunde (rechtlicher Grenzwert), ohne dass in die Pedale getreten werden muss. Praktisch an Rampen oder beim Anfahren am Berg. In Deutschland gilt für das Führen von Fahrzeugen mit Schiebehilfe Führerscheinpflicht bzw. Mofa-Prüfbescheinigungs-Pflicht.

STECKVERBINDER → sind lösbare elektrische Verbindungselemente und dienen dazu, Leistungs- und Datenkabelverbindungen herzustellen. Der beim → LEV am meisten genutzte Steckverbinder ist in der Regel der Ladestecker. Oft werden die Pole der gleichartigen Stecker aber unterschiedlich belegt, was dazu führen kann, dass versehentlich → Batterien und Ladegeräte zusammengesteckt werden, die nicht zusammengehören. So kann es zu vermeidbaren Gefahrensituationen kommen.

V → (kurz für Volt). Einheit der elektrischen Spannung. Bei → Pedelecs sind Nennspannungen von 24, 26, 32, 36 und 48 V üblich.

WH → (kurz für Wattstunde). Tatsächlicher Energiegehalt der Batterie. Produkt aus Ladung (→ Ah) und Spannung (→ V). Ein 36-V-Akku mit einer Kapazität von 10 Ah liefert Energie von 360 Wh (36 V × 10 Ah).

CREDITS

Cover collage by Sophie Franke
Back cover photos by Steve Ki, Johanna Keimeyer & Brais Gen, Travis Stanton

p 05 (Hannes Neupert) by Johanna Keimeyer

FUTURE MOBILITY (pp 06–33)
p 07 by shutterstock/leungchopan; p 09 by REUTERS/K. K. Arora; p 10 by Getty Images/ Robert Harding World Imagery; p 11 by Getty Images/Ed Pritchard; p 17 by Travis Stanton; p 19 by Hannes Neupert; pp 20–21 by Wakako Iguchi; p 22 by Patrick Knappig; p 23 by Christian Hass/Stadt Stuttgart; p 24 by Hannes Neupert; p 27 by Martin Nicholas Kunz (2); p 31 top by Julian Bückers, bottom courtesy of ExtraEnergy; p 32 by Sophie Franke

E-BIKE HISTORY (pp 34–43)
p 35 courtesy of Philips; p 37 by ExtraEnergy Archiv (top), courtesy of Mercedes Benz (middle), courtesy of patent office, USA (bottom); p 38 courtesy of Philips (top), courtesy of ExtraEnergy Archiv (middle), Hannes Neupert (bottom); p 41 courtesy of ExtraEnergy Archiv (top), Hannes Neupert (middle and bottom); p 42 by Hannes Neupert (top and bottom), courtesy of Peugeot (middle)

TECHNOLOGY (pp 44–63)
p 45 by Johanna Keimeyer and Brais Gen; p 47 by Hannes Neupert; p 48 courtesy of VSF Fahrradmanufaktur (top), Martin Jeker, Solothurn (middle), courtesy of M55 Bike (bottom); p 50 by Hannes Neupert; p 51 courtesy of Derby Cycle AG (left), Ole Jes Wittrock, ADP Engineering GmbH (middle), Hannes Neupert (right); pp 52–53 by Hannes Neupert; p 54 by Hannes Neupert; p 55 by Hannes Neupert; p 57 courtesy of Dolphin E-bikes GmbH; pp 58–59 by Hannes Neupert; p 61 courtesy of EnergyBus e.V.; pp 62–63 by 2011 Ronny Kiaulehn

10 REASONS WHY E-BIKES ARE COOL (pp 64–71)
p 65 by Travis Stanton; p 66 top by REUTERS/Alessandro Garofalo; p 66 bottom and 67 bottom by Wataru Yamamoto; p 68 by www.chang.nl (top) and Sophie Franke (bottom); p 70 by Manuel Gortez; p 71 by Maria Bobrova/iStockphoto (bottom)

PRODUCTS & PORTRAITS (pp 72–205)
p 73 by Julian Bückers; pp 74–79 (Swix Morgan Denny on Kalkhoff) by Travis Stanton; pp 80–81 courtesy of Koninklijke Gazelle N.V. (2); p 82 courtesy of Cannondale; p 83 courtesy of Bike Fun International; pp. 84–89 (Ami Konuma on Sanyo) by Wataru Yamamoto; p 90 courtesy of VSF Fahrradmanufaktur; p 91 by Thomas Geisel (4); pp 92–95 (Tyron Ricketts on e Bike Advanced Technologies GmbH) p 95 bottom by Brais Gen, others by Johanna Keimeyer; p 96 courtesy of Utopia; p 97 by Nikolaus Karlinský (3); pp 98–99 courtesy of Daimler AG (4); p 100 by Peter Godry, Düsseldorf (3); p 101 by Jürgen Amann (3); pp 102–103 by Steve Ki (4); p 104 by Markus Greber/ Kettler Bike (3); p 105 courtesy of Veloclusive, Daniel Hermann; pp 106–111 (Võ Thị Nhung on Asama) by Wakako Iguchi; p 112 courtesy of Raleigh Univega GmbH;

p 113 by Pino Petrillo/Cycle Union GmbH; p 114 courtesy of Winora Group; p 115 courtesy of www.carroux.com (3); p 116 courtesy of Solex (3); p 117 courtesy of Pantherwerke AG; pp 118–121 (Marc Feigenspan on Third Element) by Johanna Keimeyer; pp 122–123 p 123 bottom by Julian Bückers, others by Jochen Bückers (3); p 124 by Thomas Geisel; p 125 right bottom courtesy of www.carroux.com, others courtesy of Winora-Staiger GmbH (3); pp 126–127 by Till Rydyger (4); pp 128–129 courtesy of Stevens (5); pp 130–133 (Martin Braxenthaler on Otto Bock Healthcare GmbH) courtesy of Otto Bock Healthcare GmbH; pp 134–135 courtesy of Cube Bikes (5); p 136 courtesy of Giant (3); p 137 courtesy of Hercules–Accell Germany GmbH (3); pp 138–139 by Fotostudio Jahreiss (4); p 140 by Nicky Hedayat Zadeh/Stealth Electric Bikes USA LLC; p 141 courtesy of M55 Bike; pp 142–147 (Gerold Wünstel and Jayne Amelia Larson on Stromer) by Tashi Brauen; pp 148–149, p 149 top left by Sebastian Bruch, others courtesy of eRockit GmbH (3); p 150 by Martin Holzner/hoizge.de; p 151 courtesy of Biketec AG (3); p 152–153 courtesy of Dolphin E-bikes GmbH (2); pp 154–157 (Karen Grajeda on NYCeWheels) by Tashi Brauen; pp 158–159 courtesy of Mando Footloose (5); p 160 courtesy of eego e-mobiliy Gmbh (2); p 161 by Pierre Yves Le Meur (5); pp 162–163 courtesy of Karbon Kinetics Limited (4); pp 164–165 by Arnaud Lambert—visuel.ch (5); pp 166–169 (Mr. Sun on Shanghai Kaishun Double-Shoulder Loader King) by Zhifeng Xu; pp 170–171 courtesy of Juiced Riders Inc. (5); p 172 by Mandl/KTM 2013; p 173 courtesy of El Ciclo (3); p 174 by Kay Tkatzik/Riese und Müller GmbH (3); p 175 courtesy of Radkutsche; p 176 and p 177 left bottom by Michael Tewes; p 177 top and right bottom by Kay Strasser/www.kaystrasser.de; pp 178–183 (Mirko Wasic on Mifa) by Johanna Keimeyer and Brais Gen; p 184 by Werner Heyckendorff/nihola.com (5); p 185 courtesy of VanRaam (3); p 186 by Blueprint Anke Brüning; p 187 courtesy of Pacific Cycles, Inc.; pp 188–189 by Dominik Stixenberger/www.dphoto.at (4); pp 190–195 (Norbert Haller on A2B) by Johanna Keimeyer and Brais Gen; p 196 courtesy of Porsche Design Group; p 197 courtesy of BMW AG (2); p 198 courtesy of Audi AG (2); p 199 courtesy of Ford-Werke GmbH; p 200 courtesy of Toyota; p 201 by Axel Wierdemann (left), all courtesy of Opel AG; p 202 by Hannes Neupert (3); p 203 courtesy of Yuji Fujimura (3); pp 204–205 by Max Tomasinelli/www.maxtomasinelli.com (4)

RIGHT BIKE FOR YOUR TYPE (pp 206–211)
p 207 courtesy of El Ciclo

Illustrations on p 15 (top), p 49, p 67 (top) based on graphics by Moritz Grünke, büro pluspunkt. Illustration on p 60 based on graphic by Atelier Papenfuss, Weimar. Illustration on p 71 (top) based on graphic by Sanyo.

Special thanks to:
NYCeWheels (www.nycewheels.com) and Peter Yuskauskas; IZIP Store, Santa Monica (www.izipstore.com); Electric Bikes LA (www.electricbikesla.com) and Andrea Busch; Green Light Bikes, Portland (www.greenlightbikes.com) and Todd Peres.

IMPRINT

Introduction: Hannes Neupert
Texts: Hannes Neupert, Juliane Schröder, Marisa Schulz
Translations: WeSwitch Languages
Heather B. Bock, Romina Russo Lais, Heidi Holzer (English), Romina Russo Lais (German)
Copy Editing: Seamus Mullarkey (English), Claudia Jürgens, Dr. Simone Bischoff (German)
Editorial Coordination: Regine Freyberg, Johanna Keimeyer, Juliane Schröder
Creative Direction: Martin Nicholas Kunz
Layout, Prepress, Illustrations: Sophie Franke
Photo Shoot Coordination: Johanna Keimeyer
Photo Editing: David Burghardt
Imaging: Tridix, Berlin; David Burghardt
Production: Alwine Krebber

Published by teNeues Publishing Group
teNeues Verlag GmbH + Co. KG
Am Selder 37, 47906 Kempen, Germany
Phone: +49 (0)2152 916 0, Fax: +49 (0)2152 916 111
e-mail: books@teneues.de

Press Department: Andrea Rehn
Phone: +49 (0)2152 916 202
e-mail: arehn@teneues.de

teNeues Digital Media GmbH
Kohlfurter Straße 41–43, 10999 Berlin, Germany
Phone: +49 (0)30 700 77 65 0

teNeues Publishing Company
7 West 18th Street, New York, NY 10011, USA
Phone: +1 212 627 9090, Fax: +1 212 627 9511

teNeues Publishing UK Ltd.
12 Ferndene Road, London SE24 0AQ, UK
Phone: +44 (0)20 3542 8997

teNeues France S.A.R.L.
39, rue des Billets, 18250 Henrichemont, France
Phone: +33 (0)2 4826 9348, Fax: +33 (0)1 7072 3482

www.teneues.com
© 2013 teNeues Verlag GmbH + Co. KG, Kempen

ISBN: 978-3-8327-9701-0
Library of Congress Control Number: 2013930382
Printed in Czech Republic

MIX
Papier aus verantwortungsvollen Quellen
Paper from responsible sources
FSC® C005833
FSC
www.fsc.org